My Baby's First Big Activity Book: Math & Phonics

TEACH, LEARN, & GROW

PHONICS

FIVE VOWELS

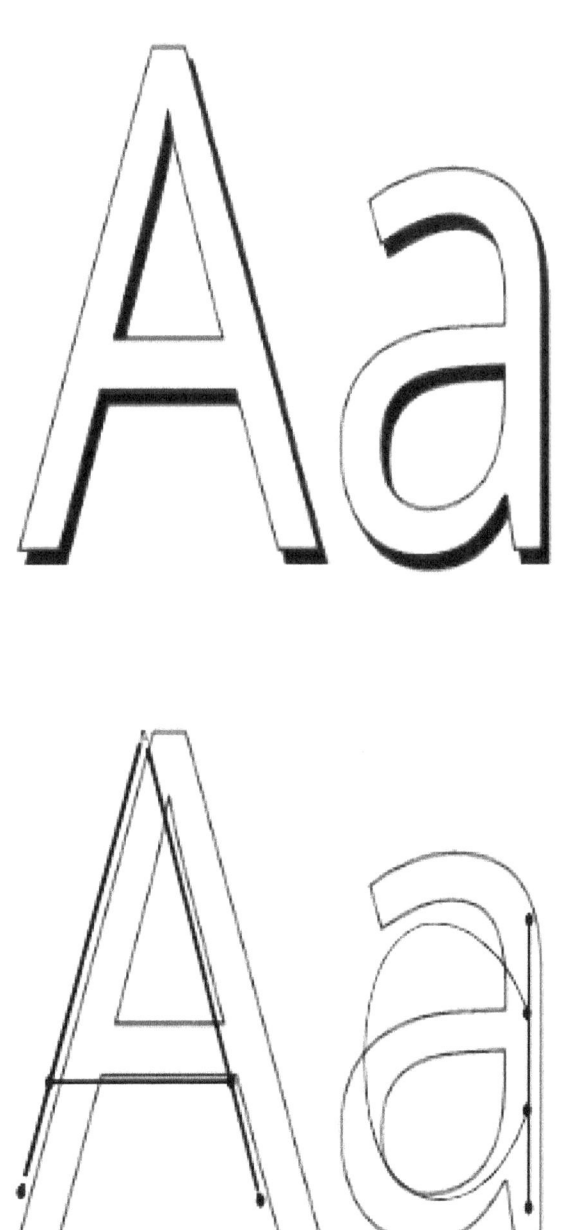

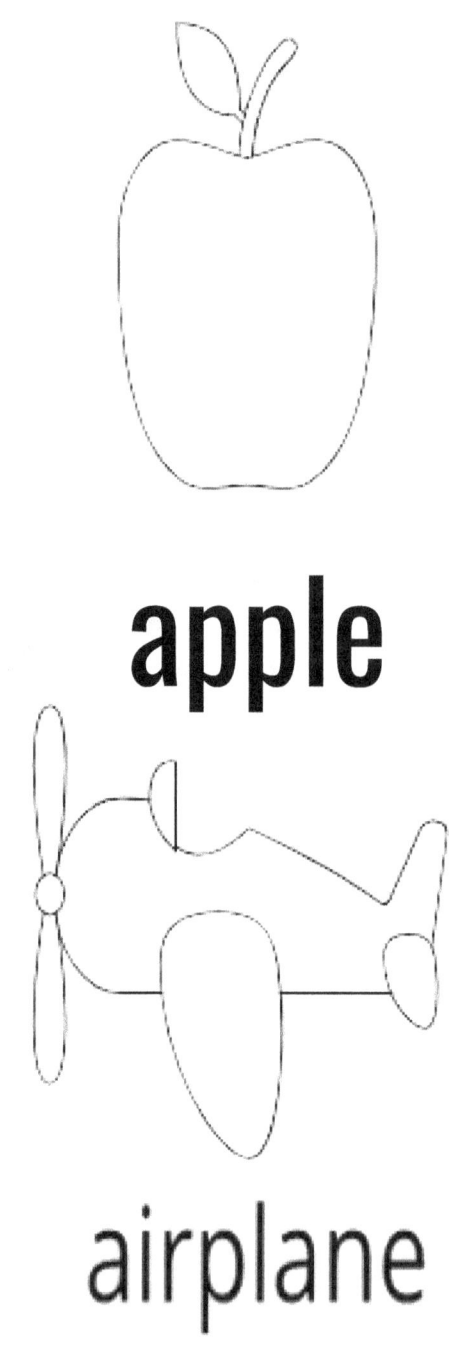

apple

airplane

COLORFUL SHORT VOWELS

Short a

Say the name of each picture. Color the picture in each row that has the Short a vowel sound.

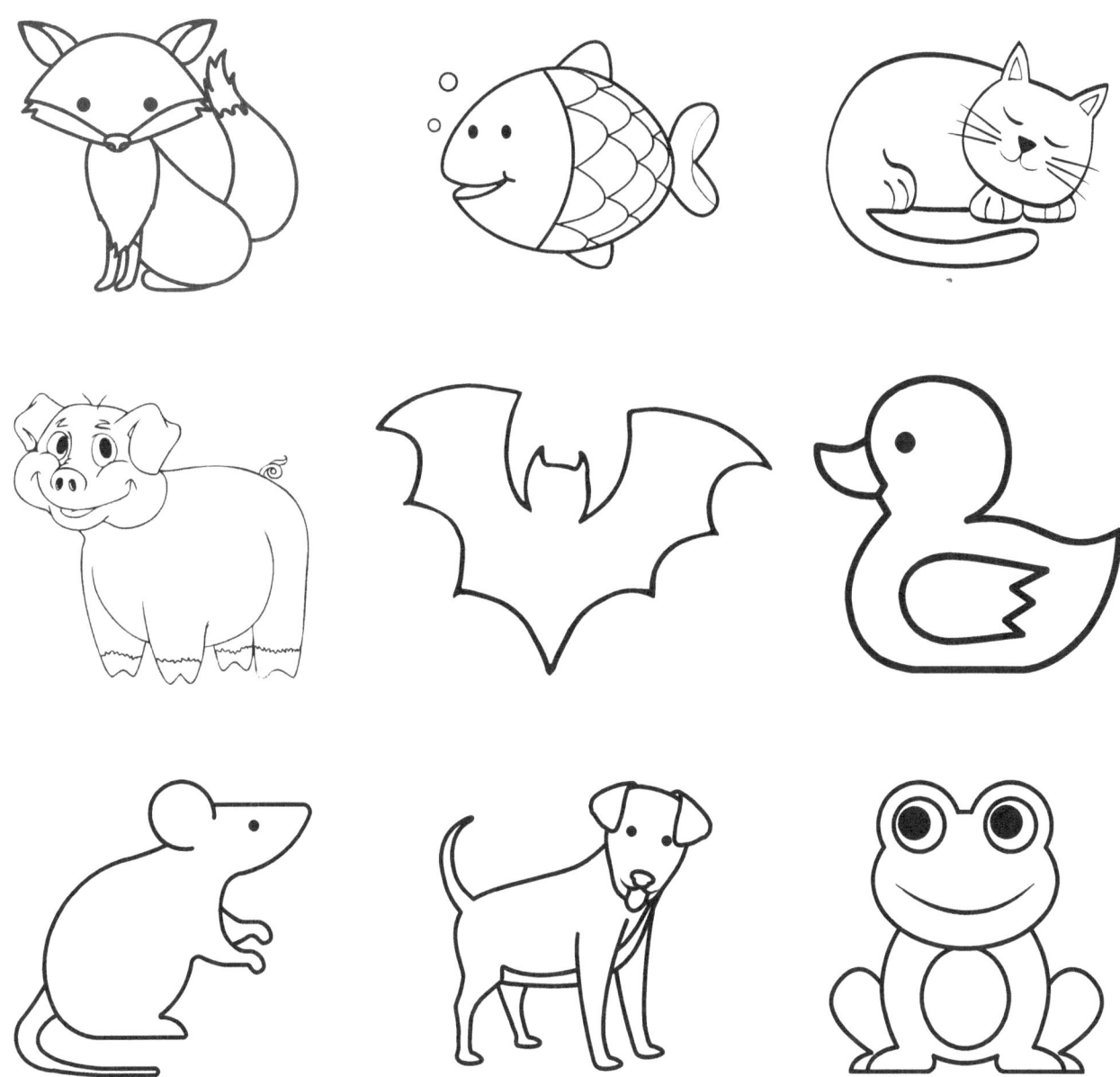

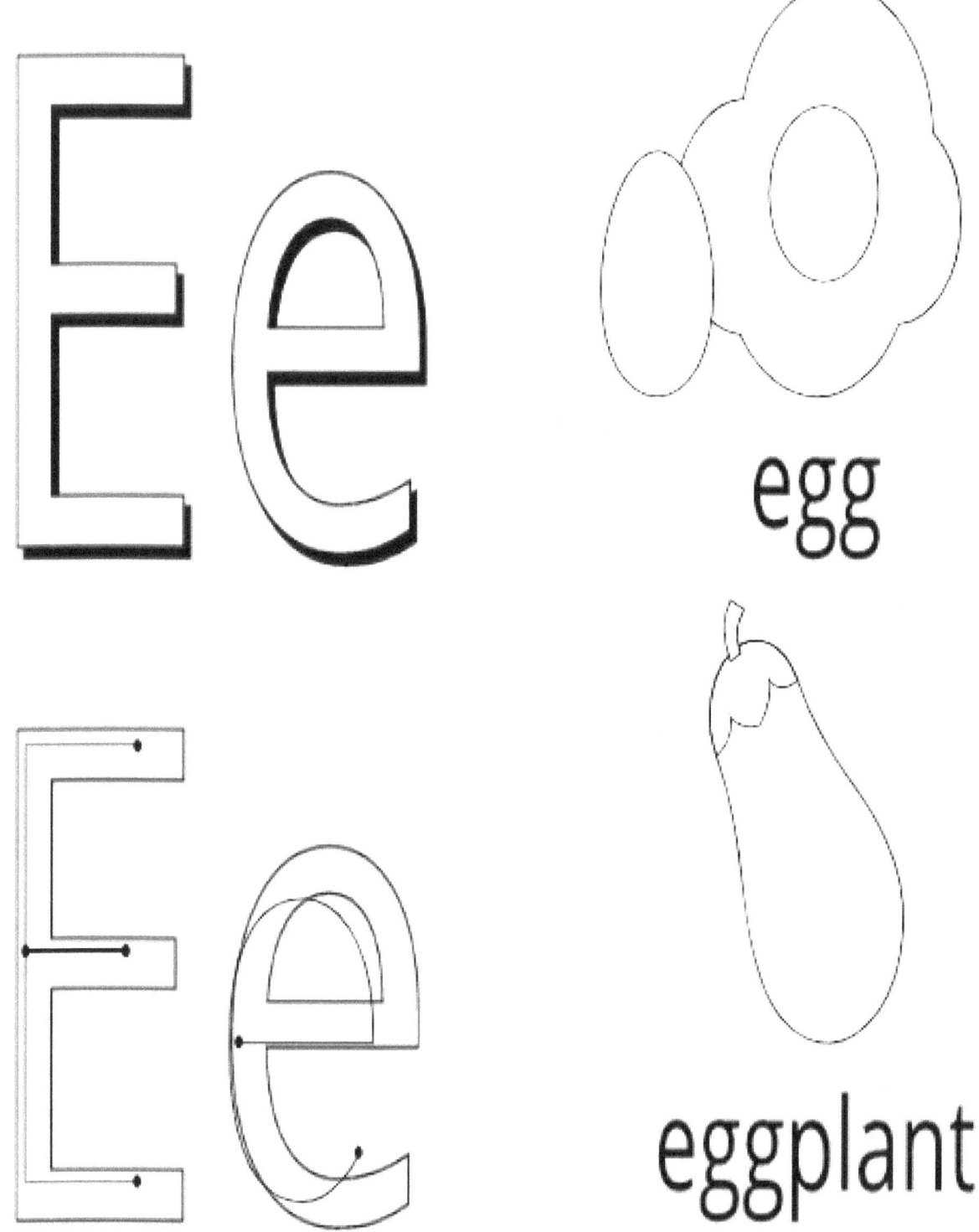

egg

eggplant

COLORFUL SHORT VOWELS

Short e

Say the name of each picture. Color the picture in each row that has the Short e vowel sound.

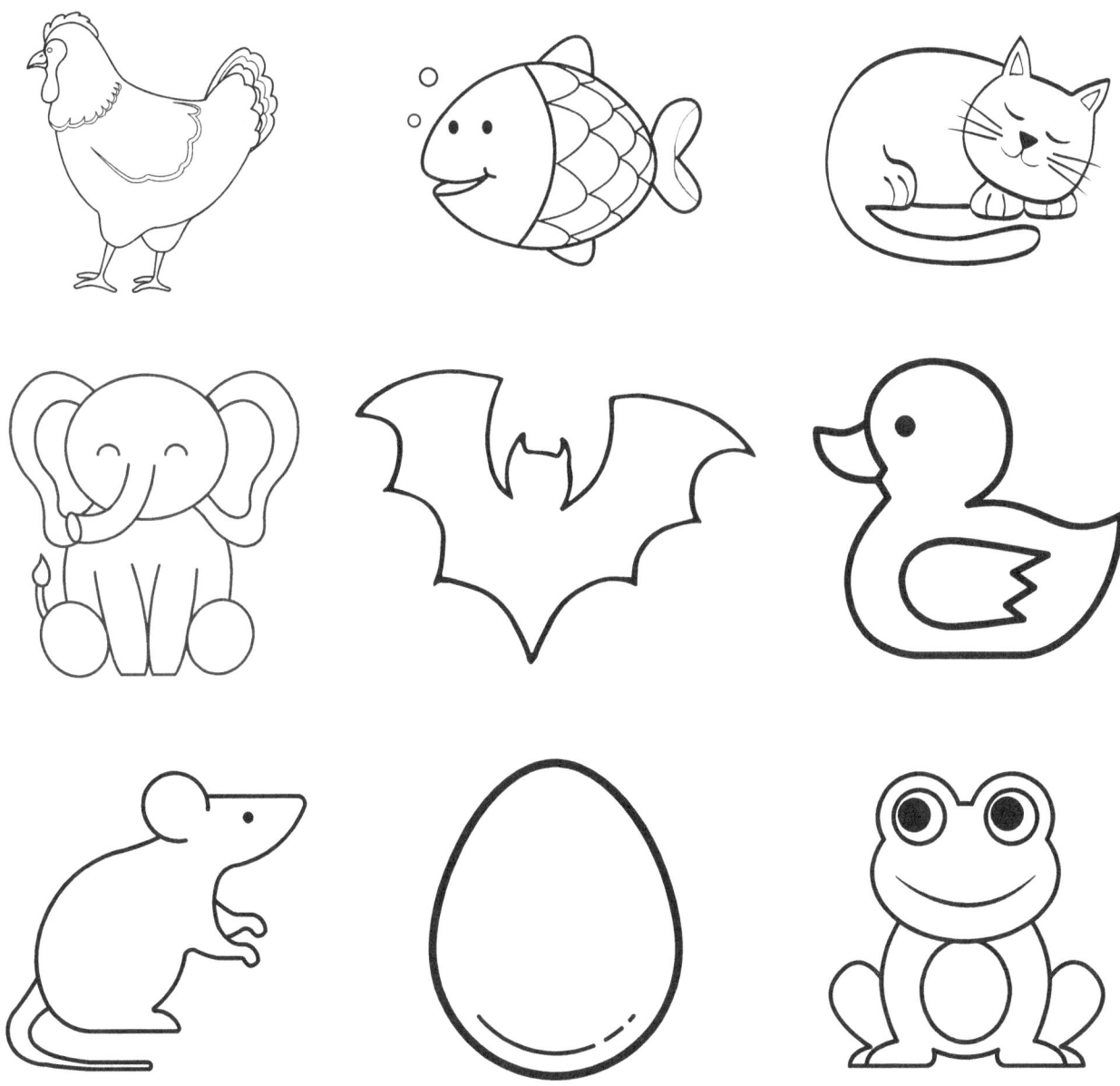

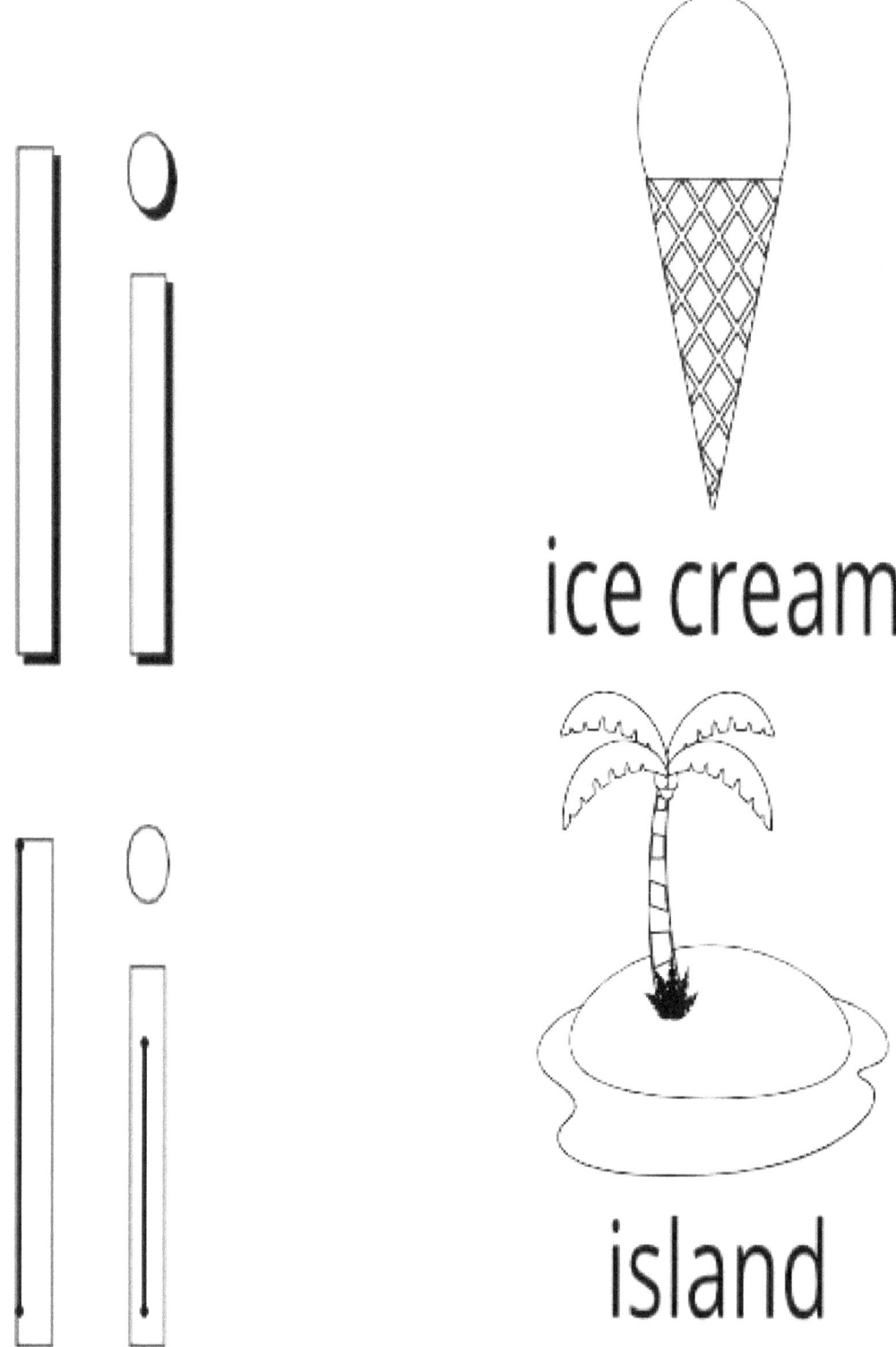

ice cream

island

COLORFUL SHORT VOWELS

Short i

Say the name of each picture. Color the picture in each row that has the Short i vowel sound.

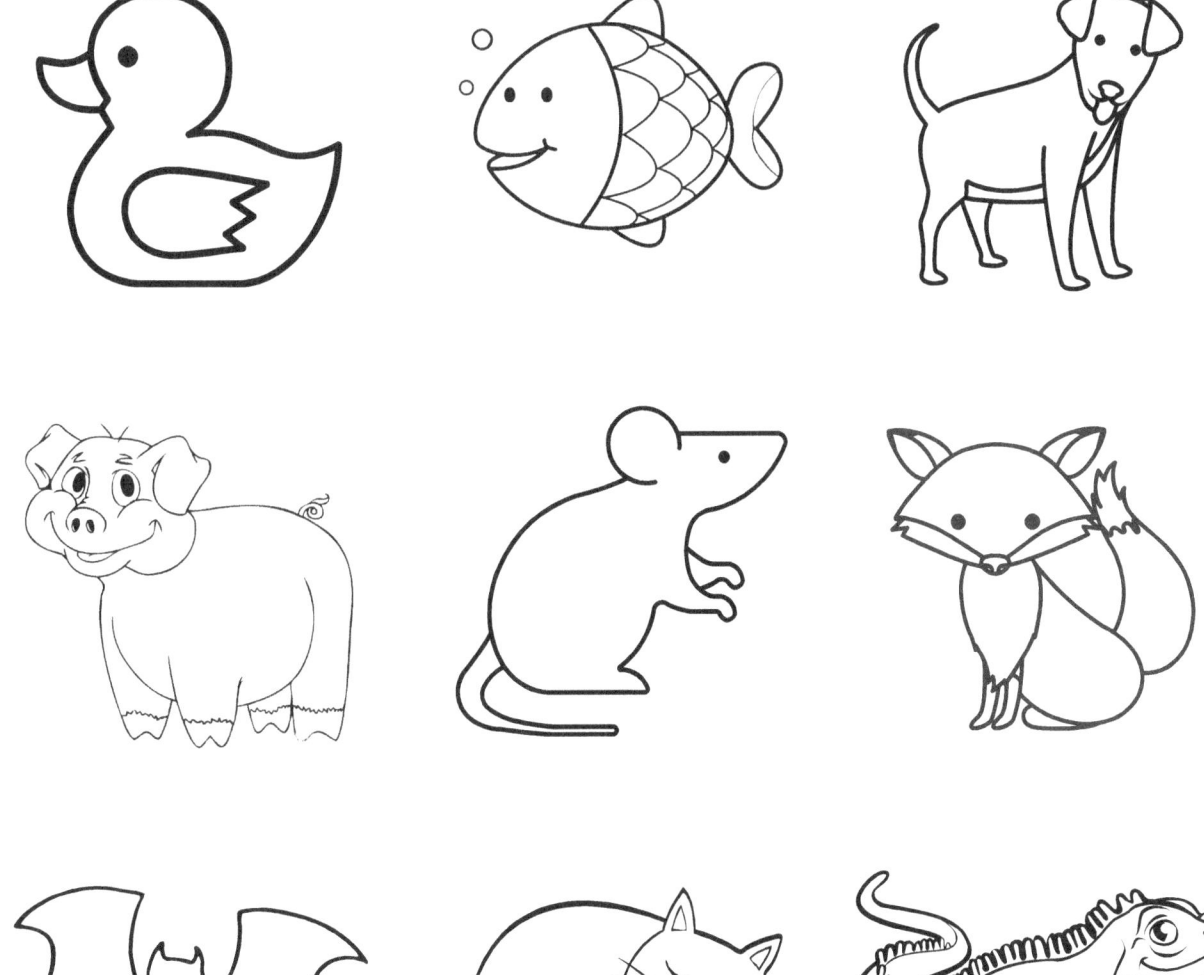

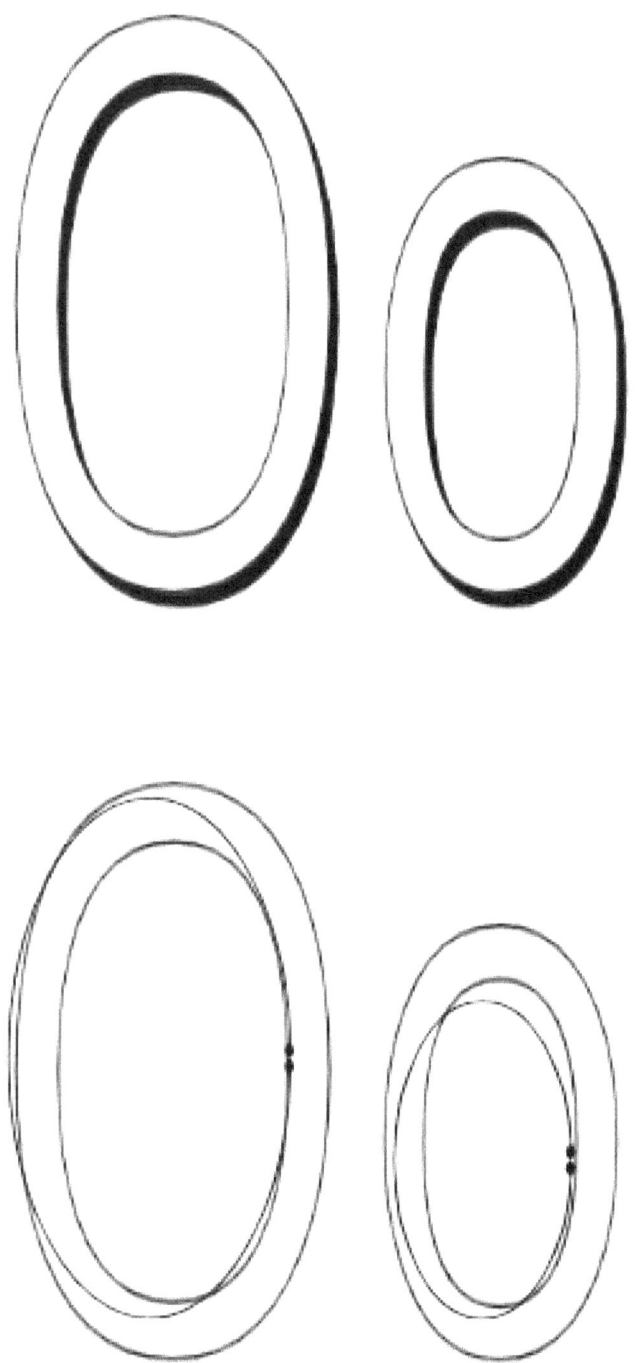

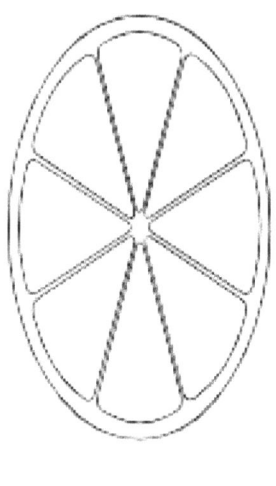

orange

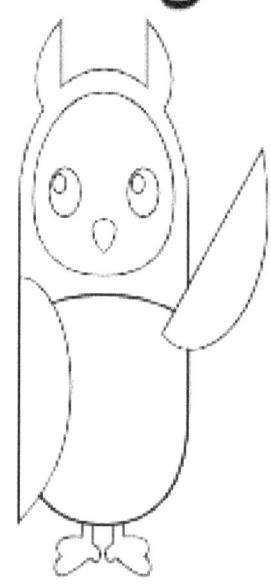

owl

COLORFUL SHORT VOWELS

Short o

Say the name of each picture. Color the picture in each row that has the Short o vowel sound.

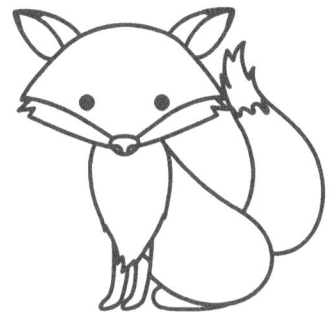 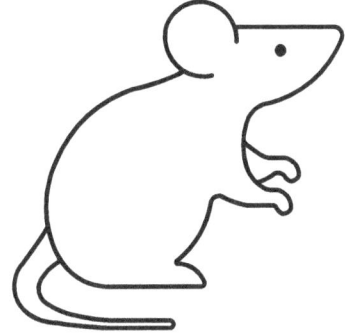 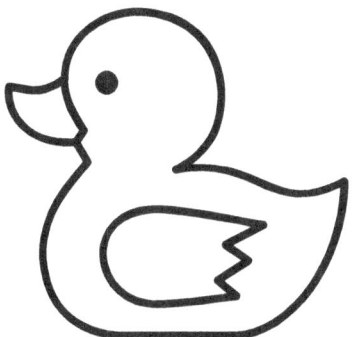

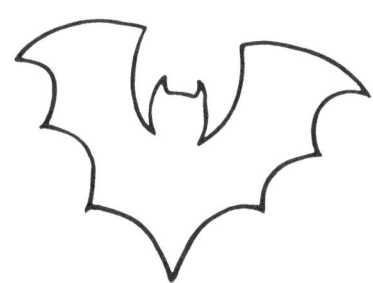 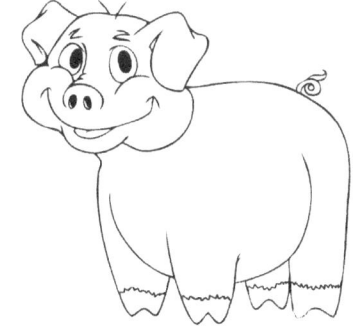 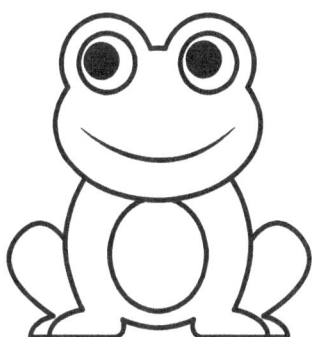

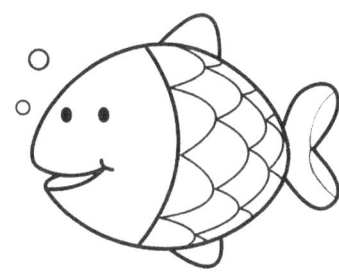 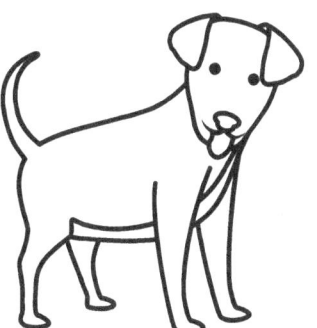 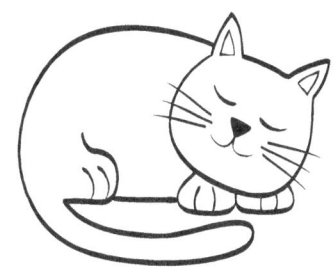

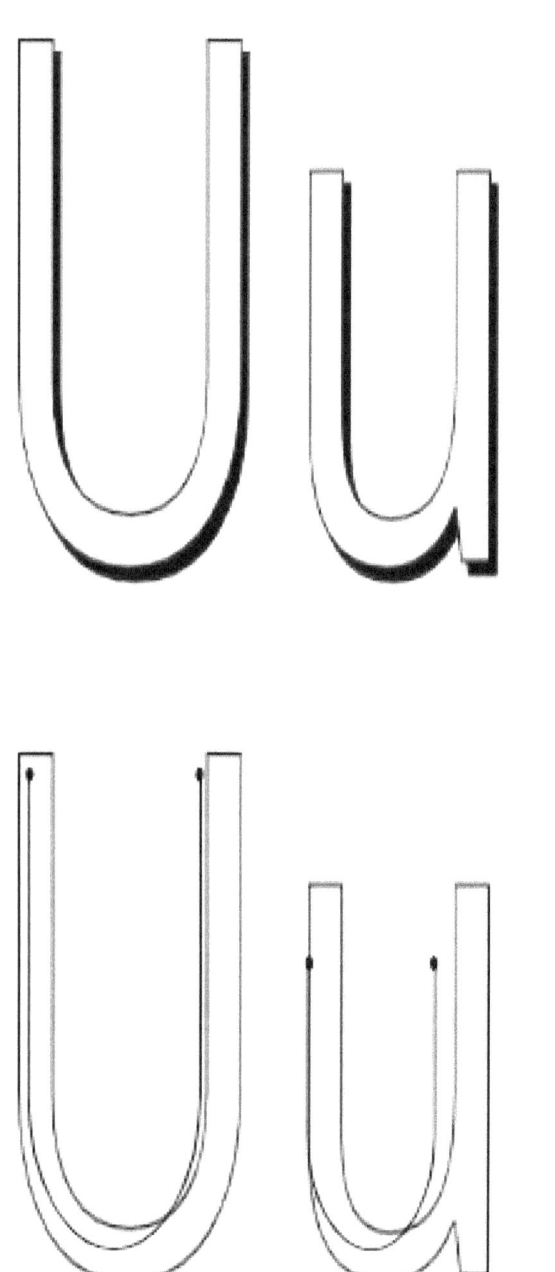

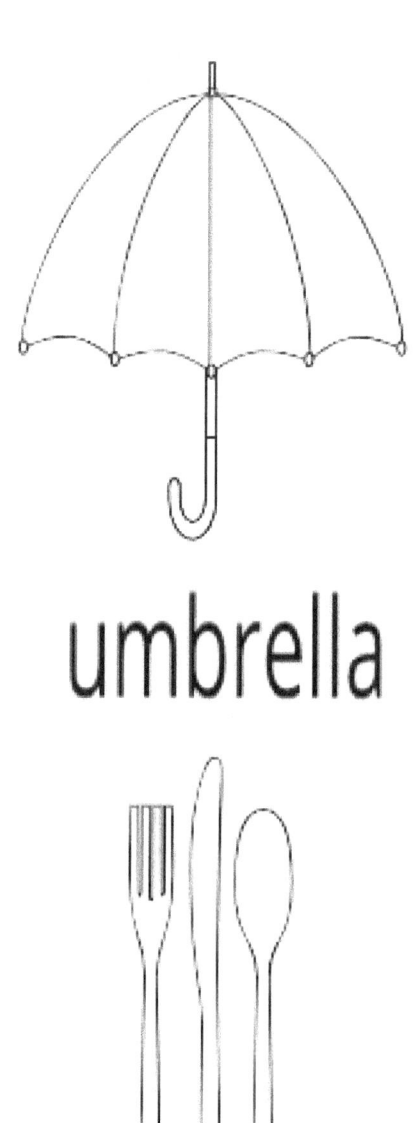

umbrella

utensil

COLORFUL SHORT VOWELS

Short u

Say the name of each picture. Color the picture in each row that has the Short u vowel sound.

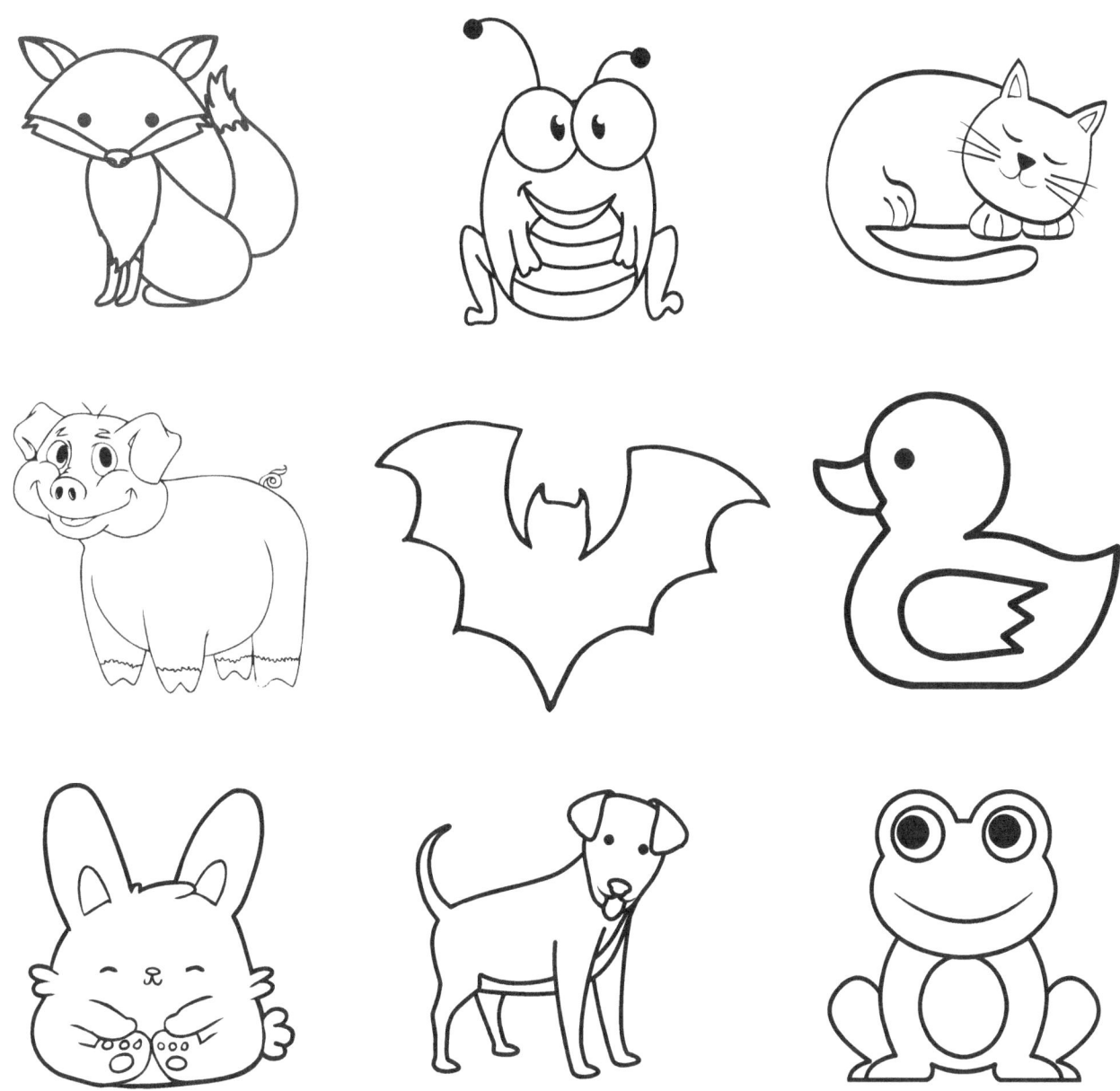

On the Farm

Cow

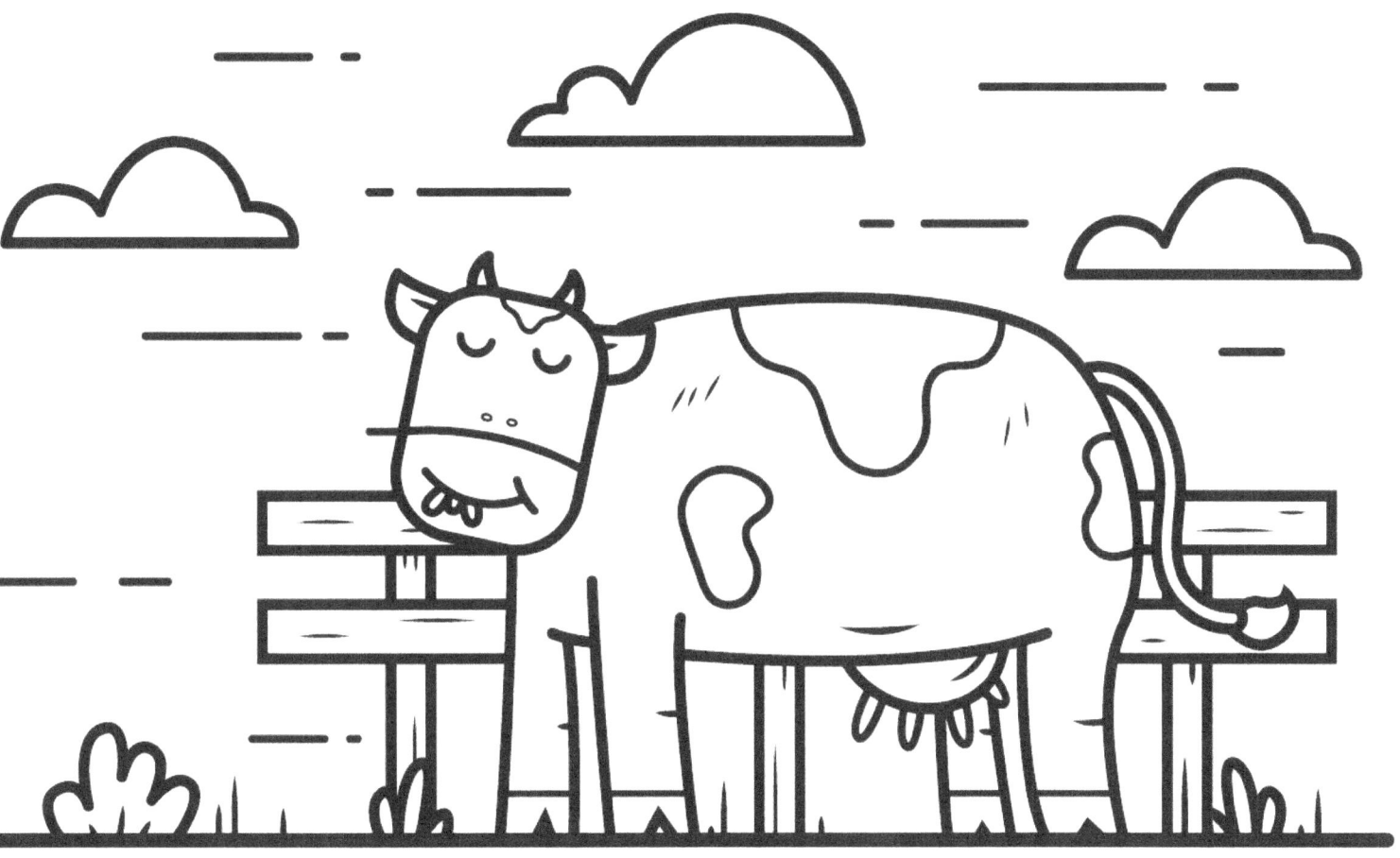

horse

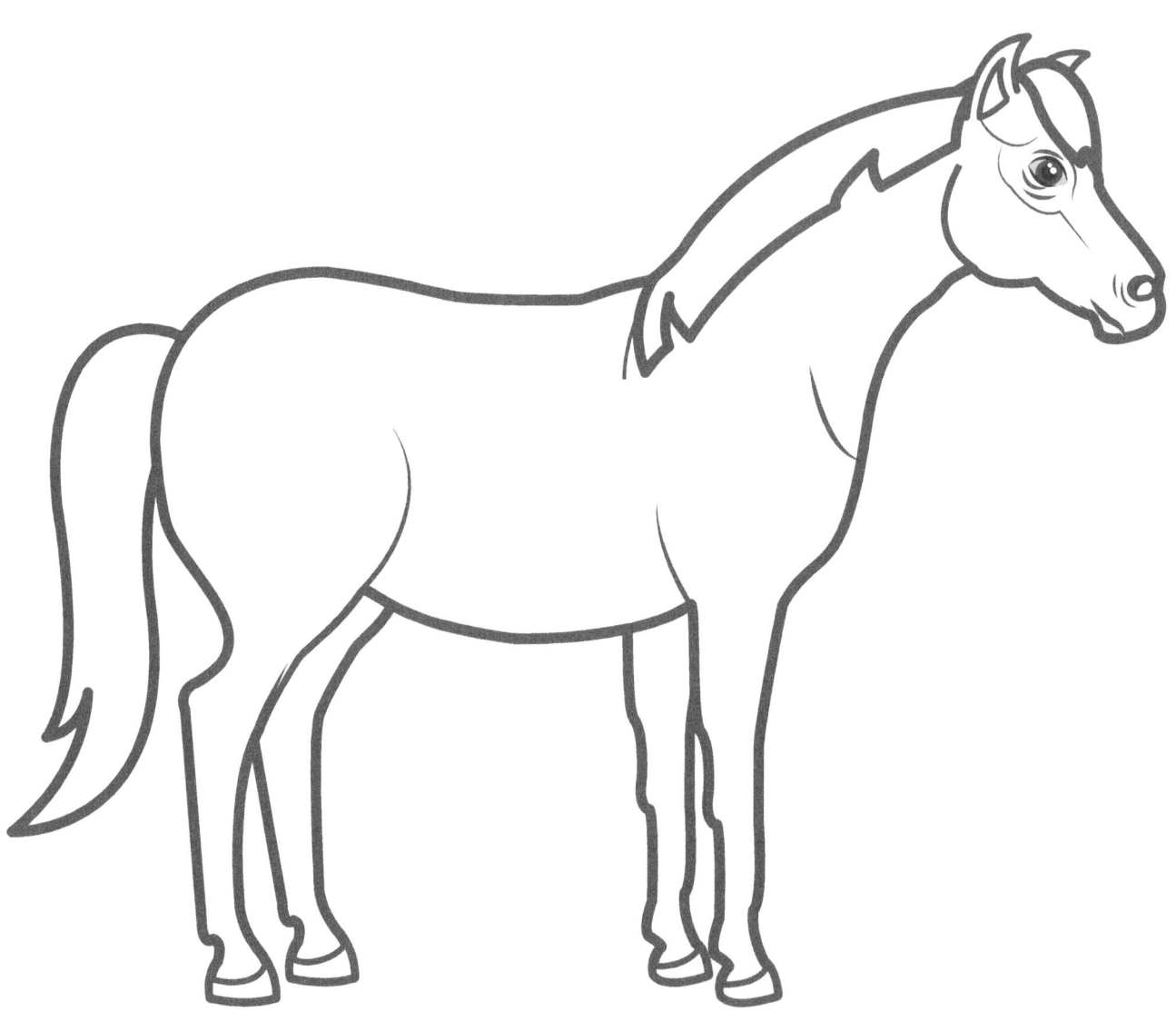

pig

goat

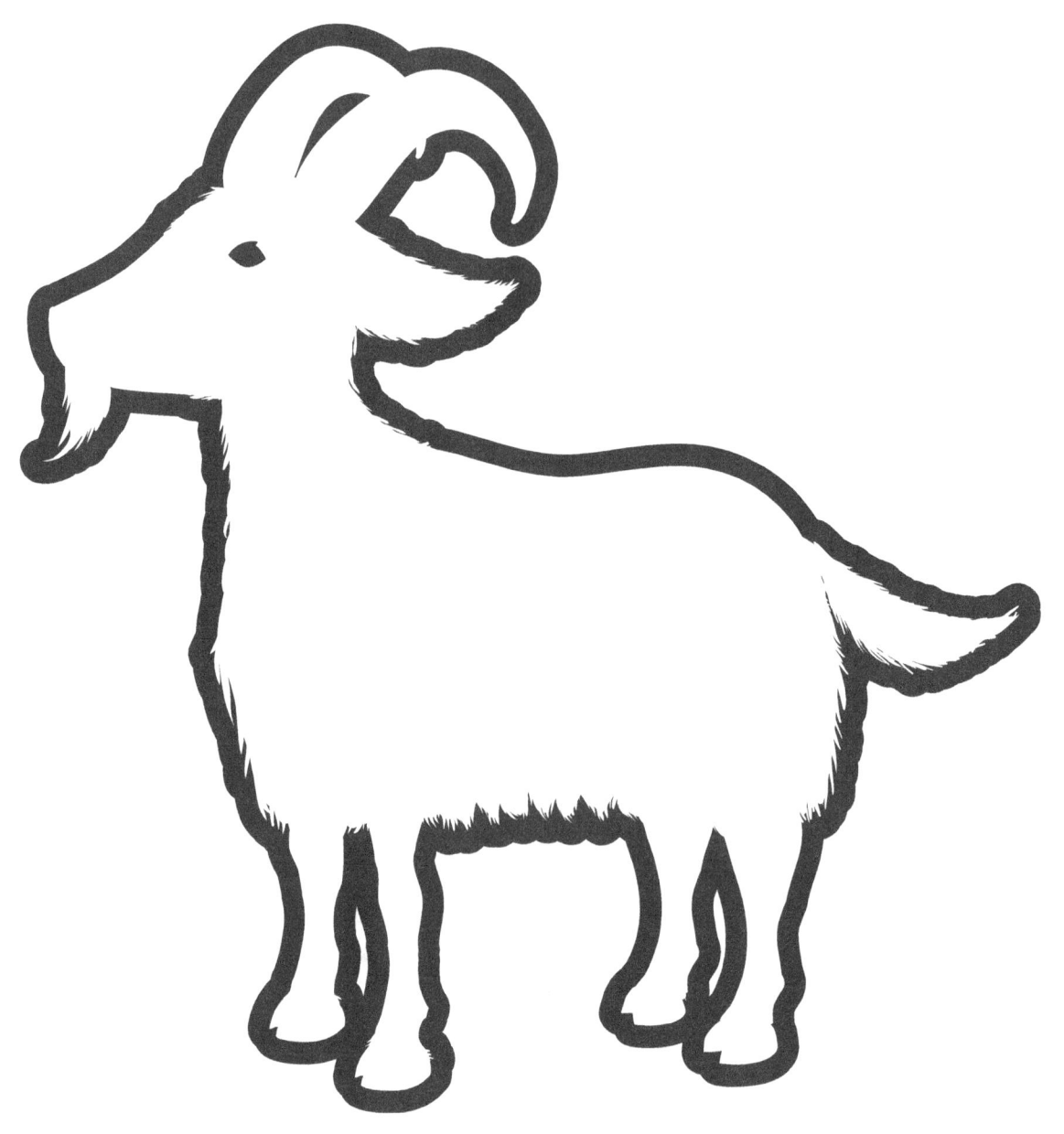

duck

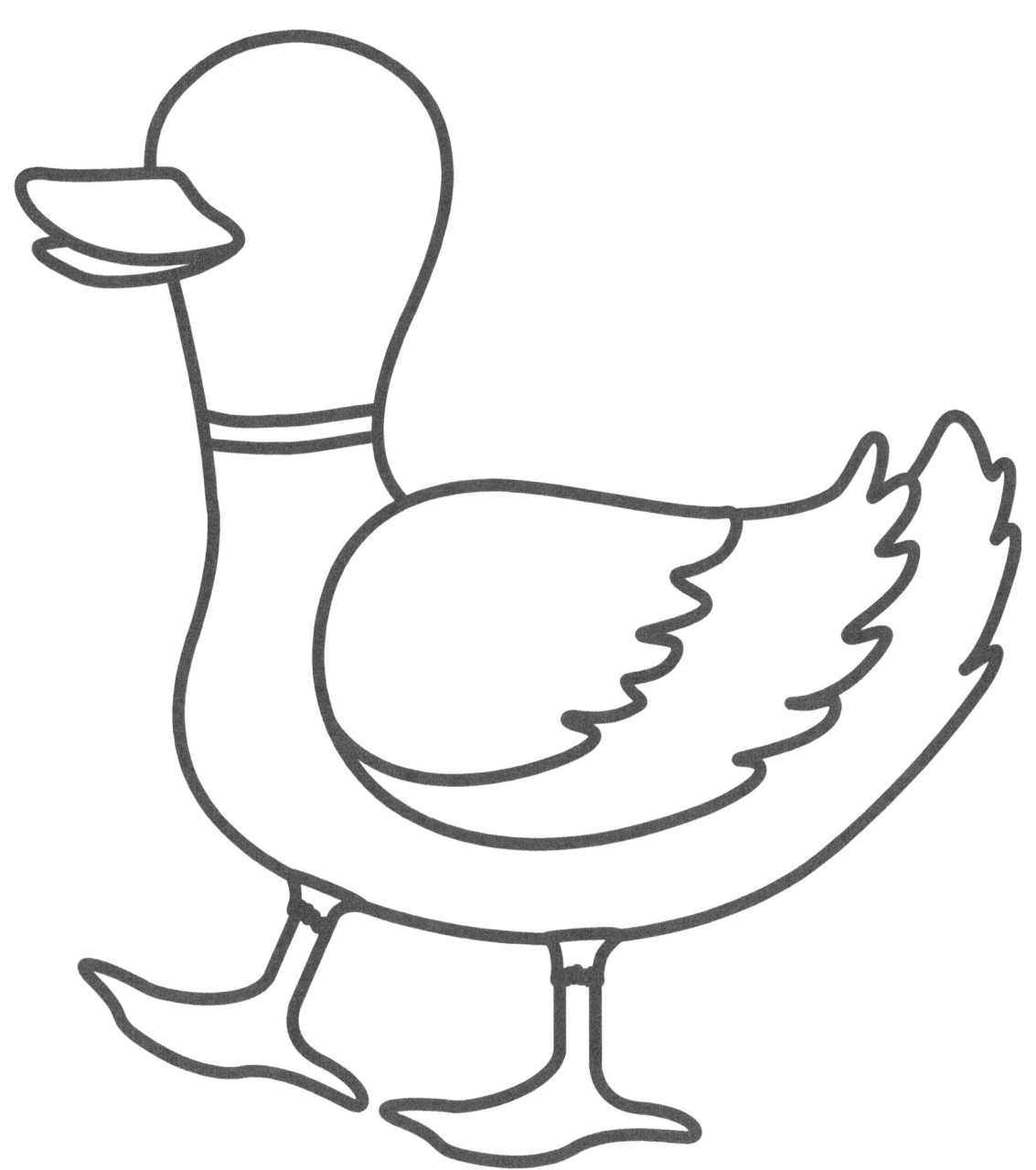

Chicken

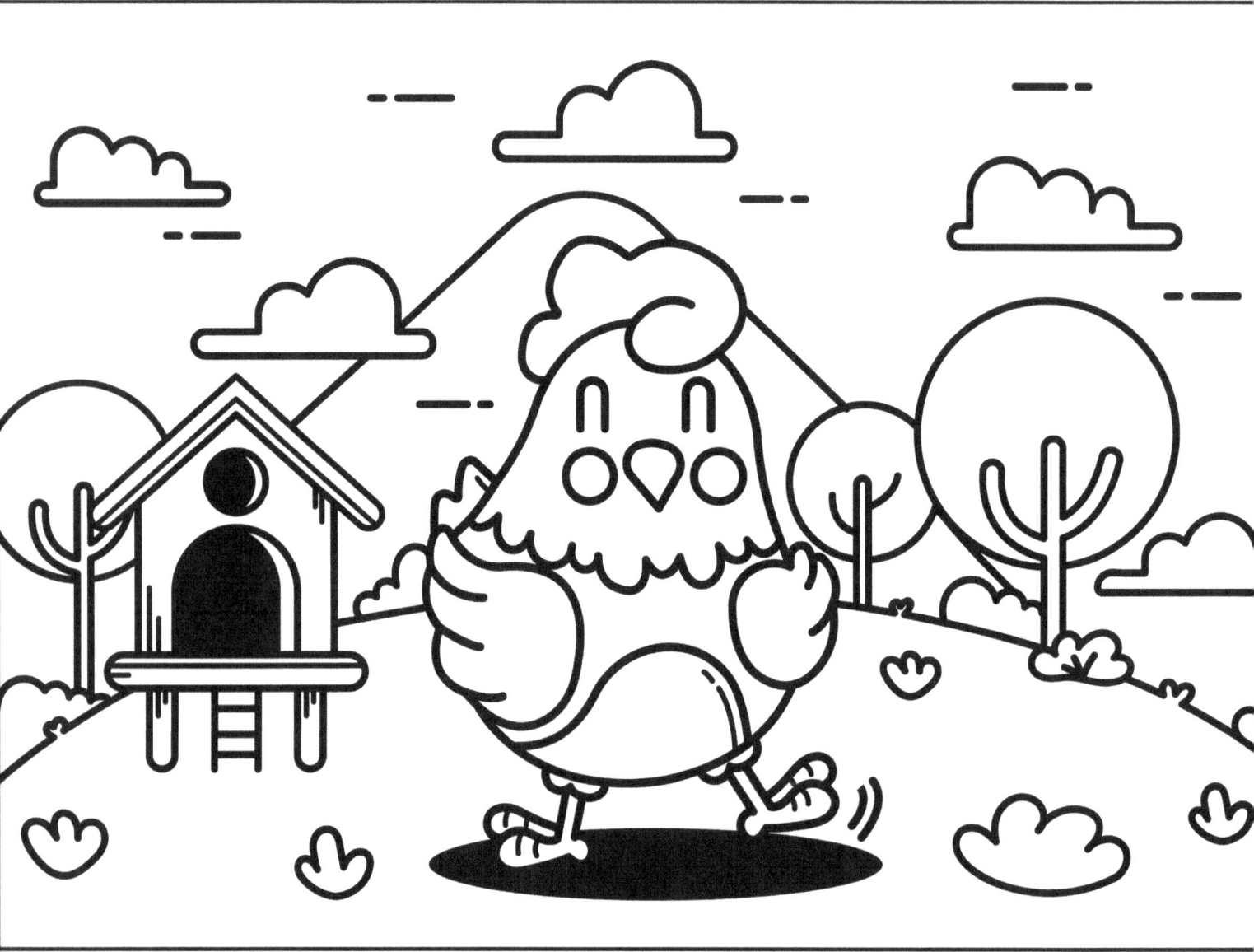

Farm

ADD THE ANIMALS ON THE FARM

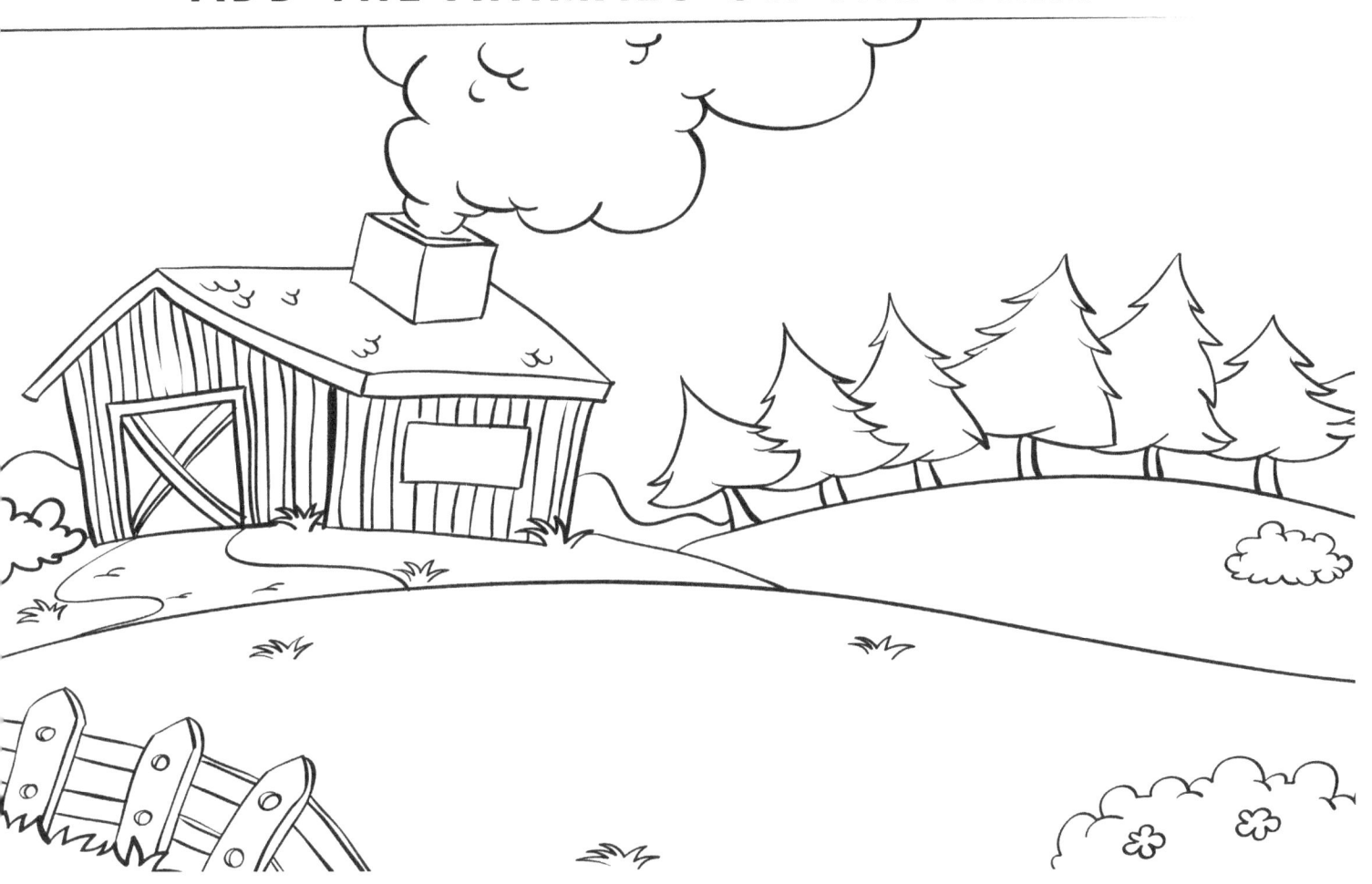

Farm Animal
Color the farm animals

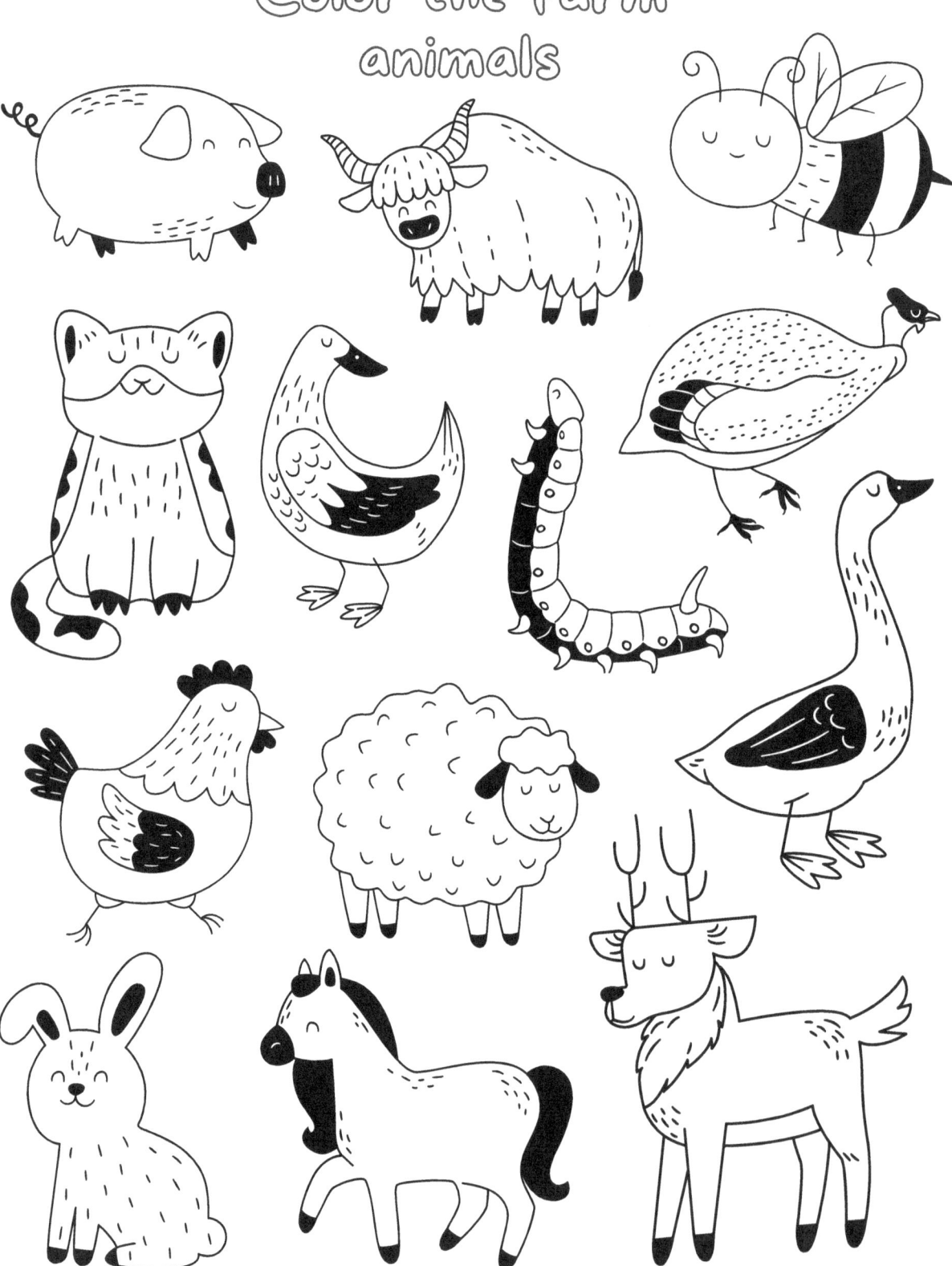

Numbers 1-10

COLOR SHEETS

1 1

One

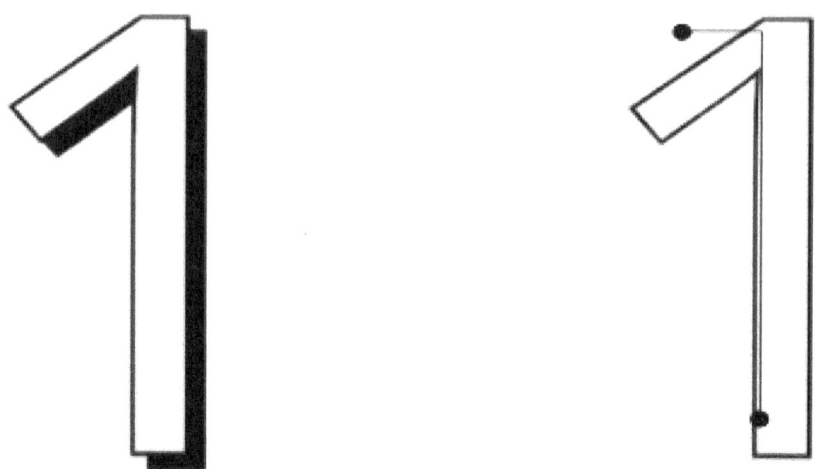

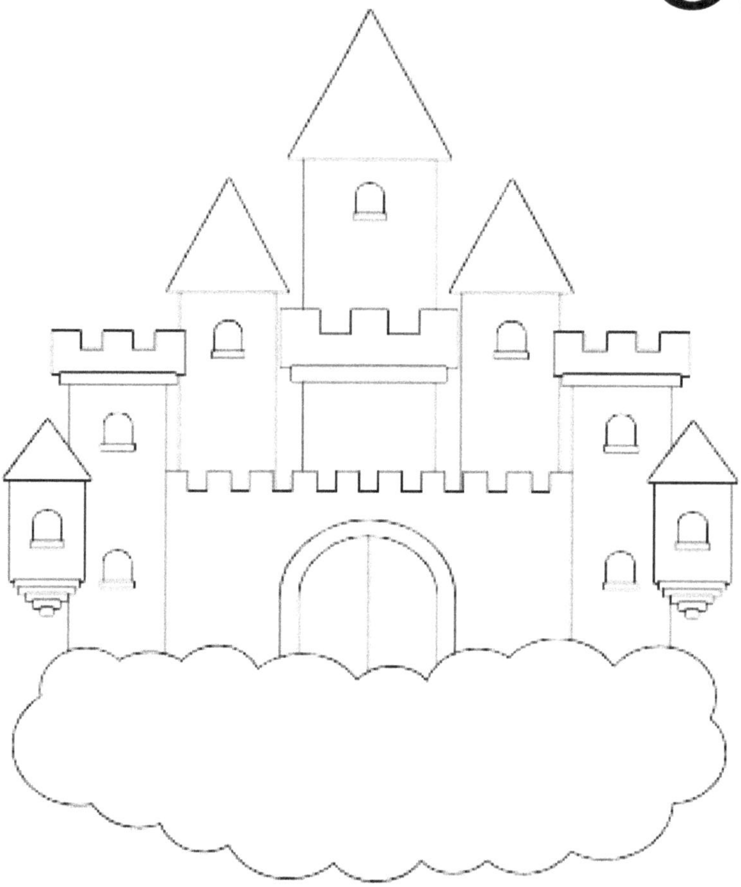

The Number One

DIRECTIONS: TRACE THE WORDS AND NUMBERS BELOW TO PRACTICE THE NUMBER ONE! WHEN YOU'RE FINISHED COLOR THE NUMBER.

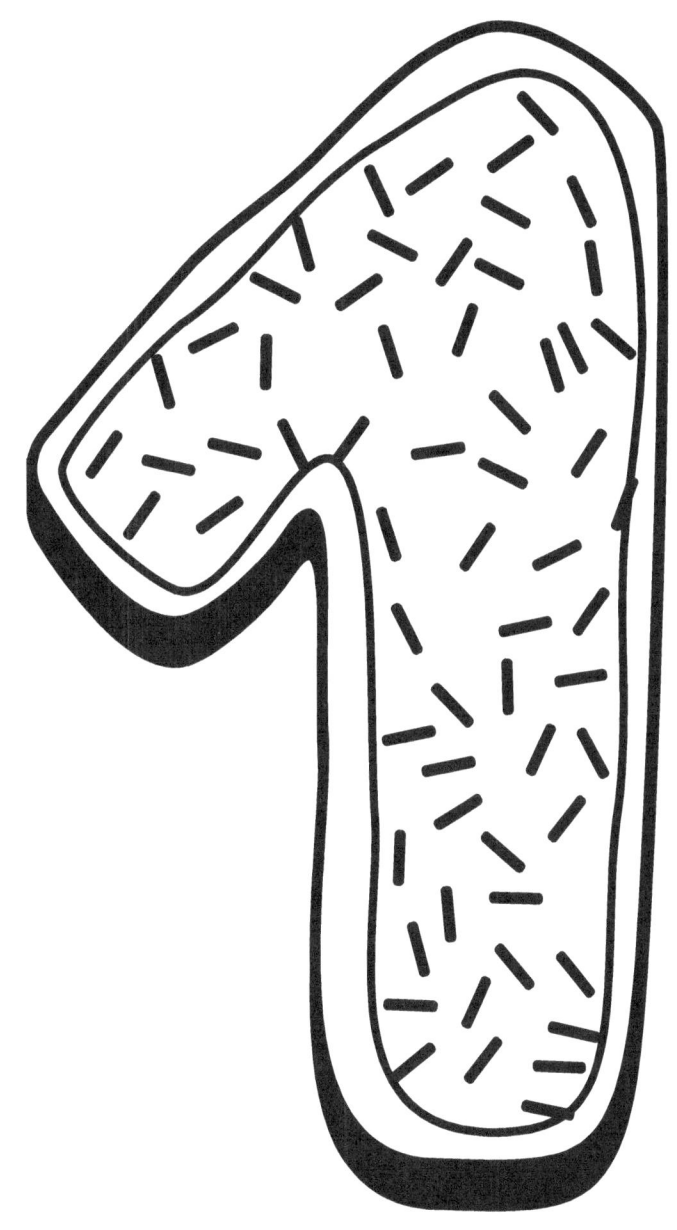

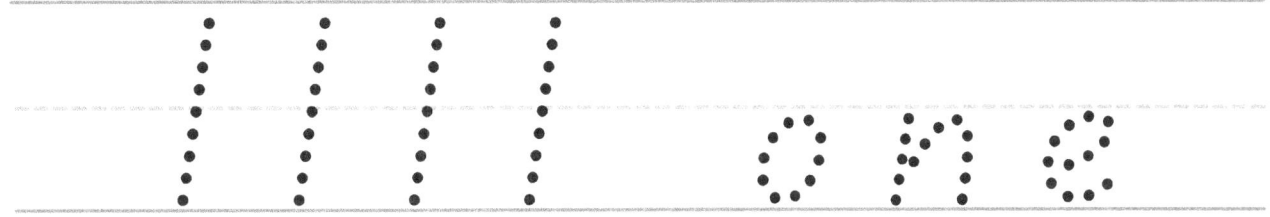

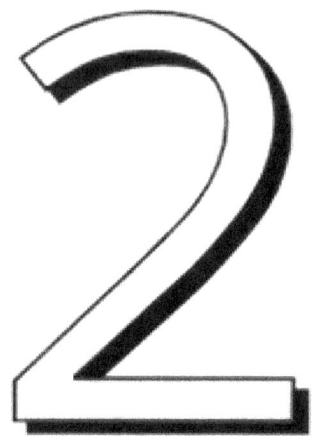 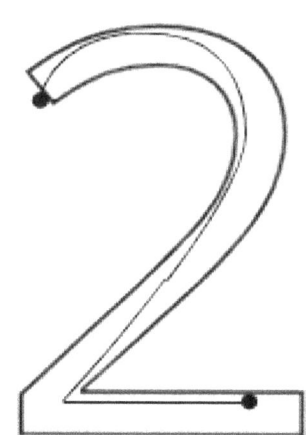

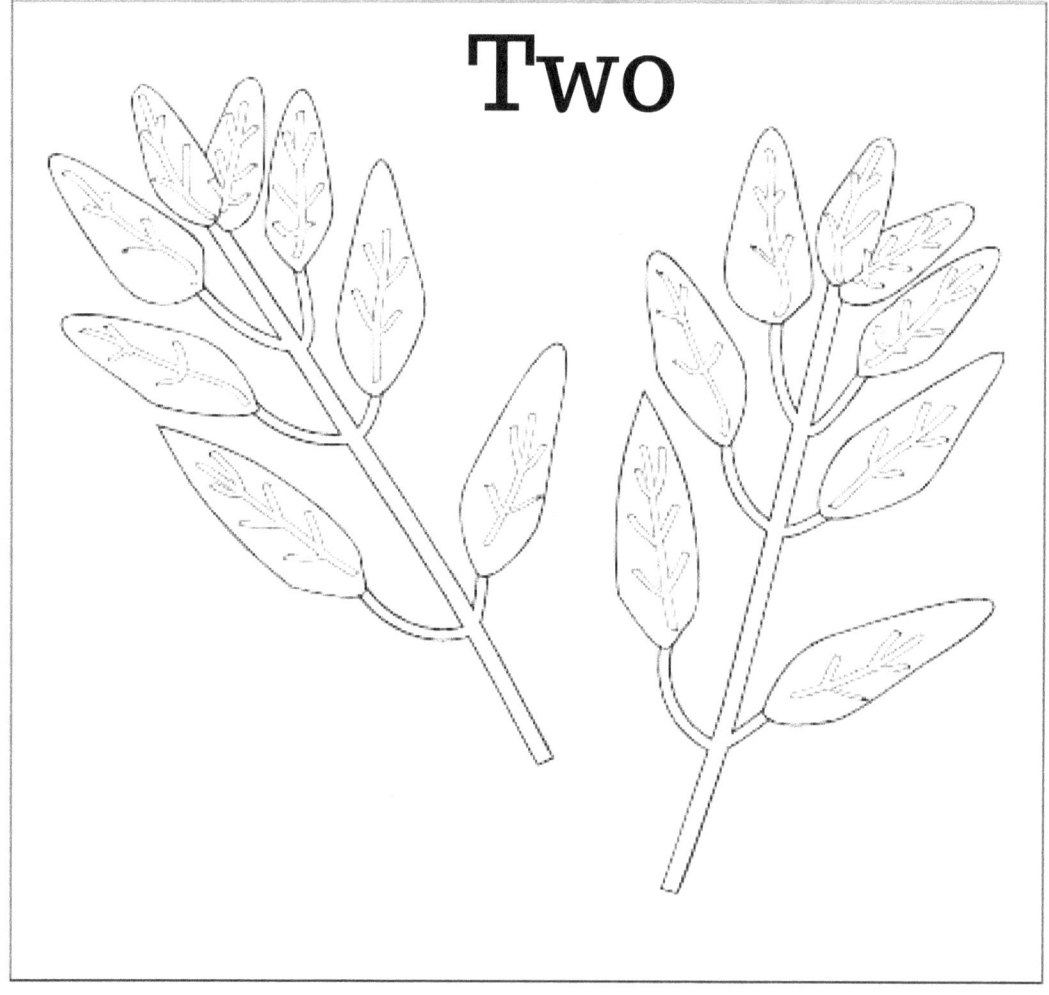

Two

DIRECTIONS: TRACE THE WORDS AND NUMBERS BELOW.

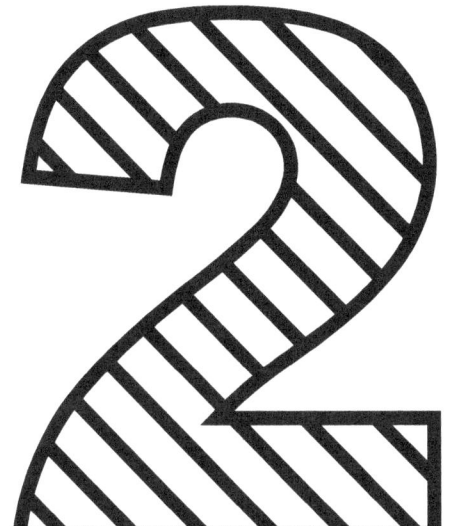

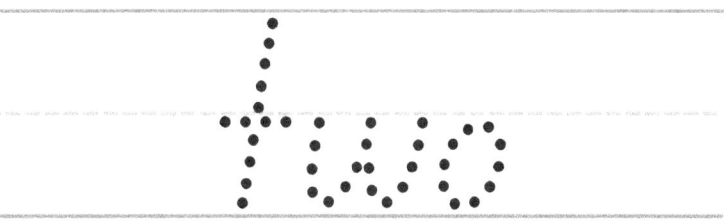

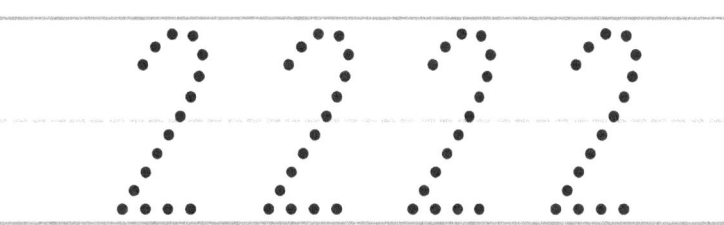

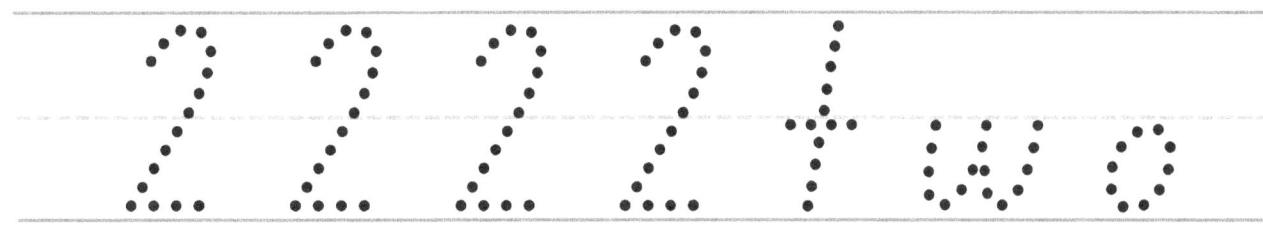

COLOR TWO TRIANGLES:	CIRCLE THE TWOS:

COLOR TWO TRIANGLES:

CIRCLE THE TWOS:

2	3	5
4	2	1
6	1	2
1	2	1
2	1	4

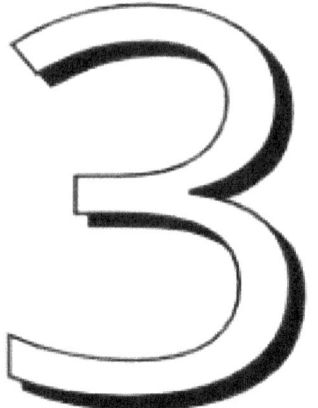 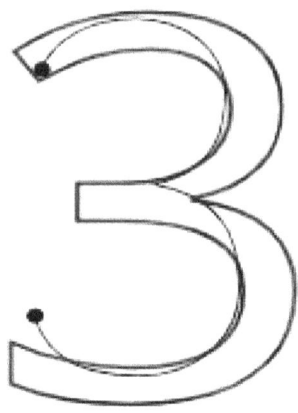

Three

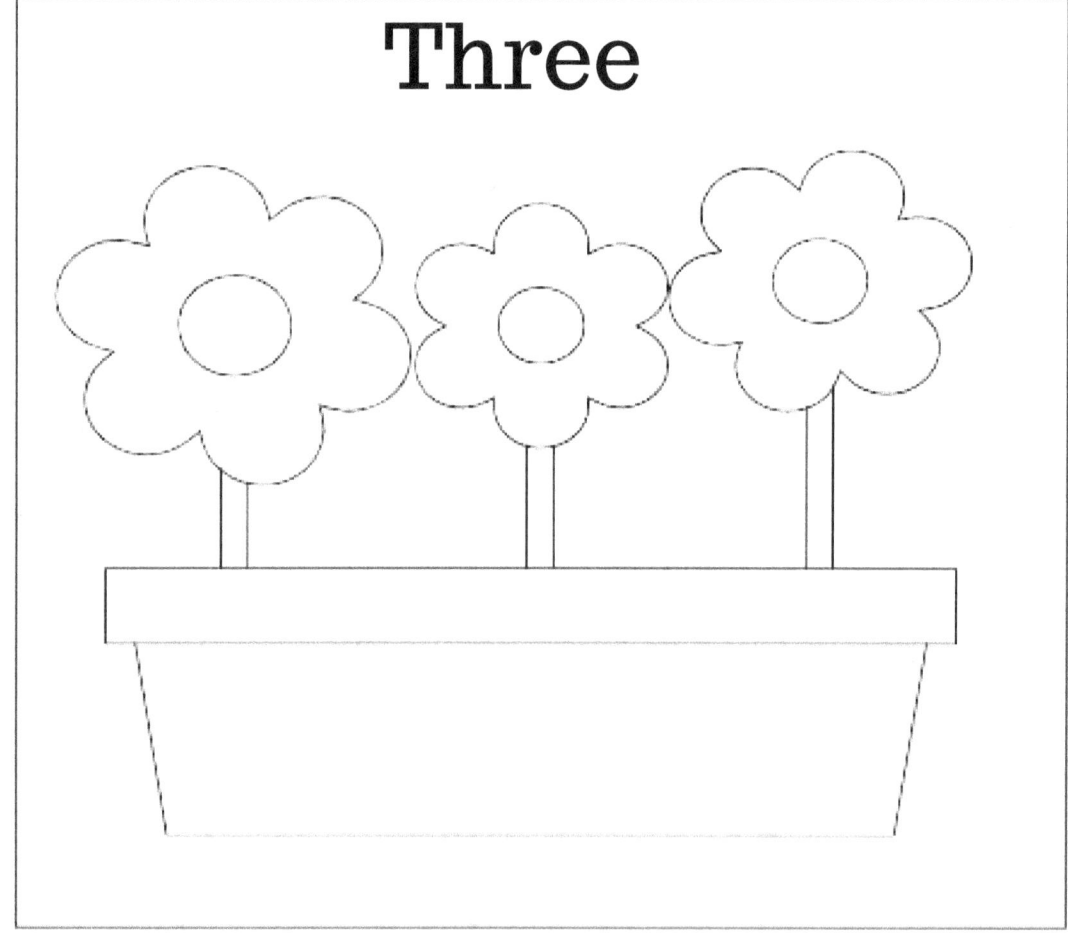

Name: _____

DIRECTIONS: TRACE THE WORDS AND NUMBERS BELOW.

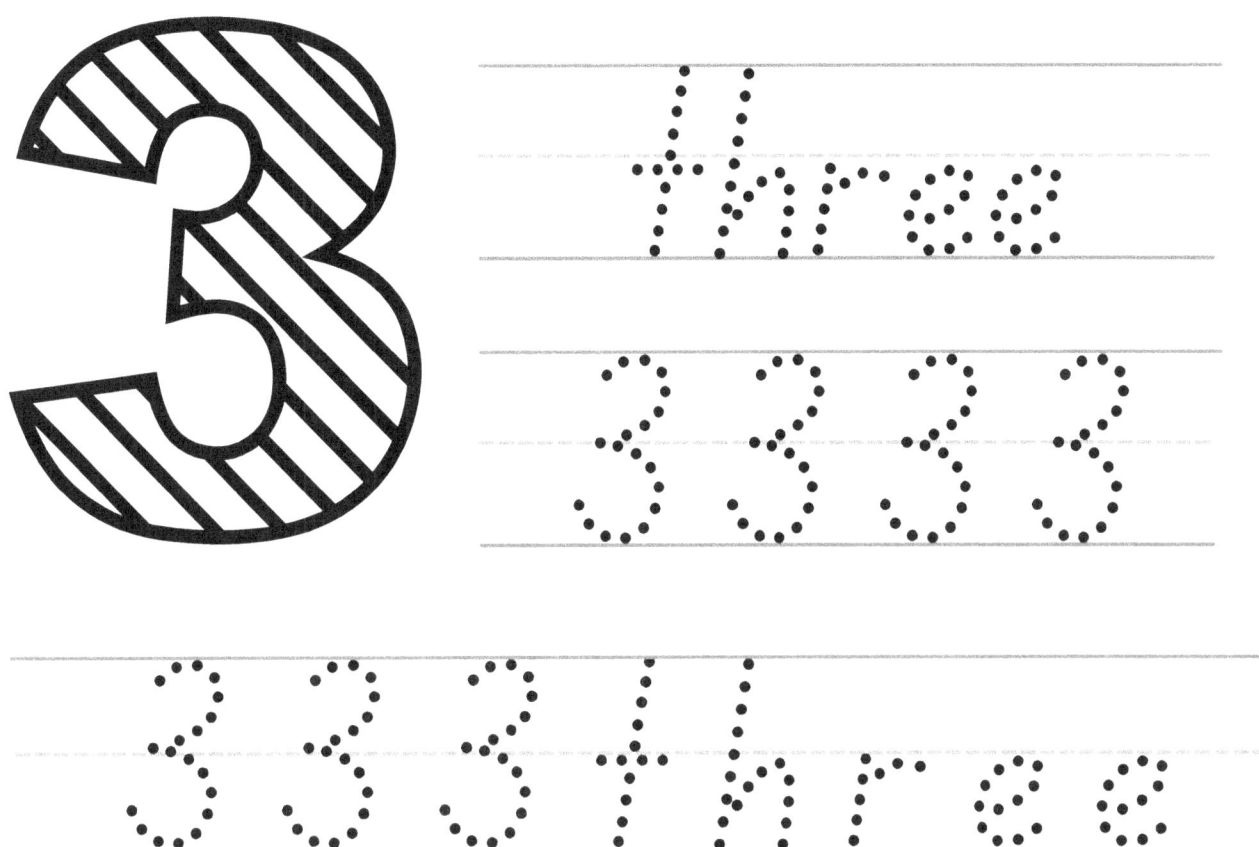

three

3 3 3 3

3 3 3 three

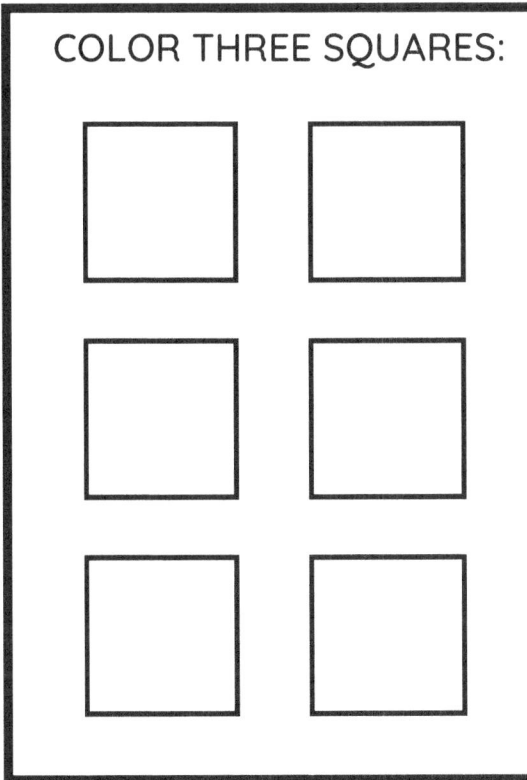

COLOR THREE SQUARES:

CIRCLE THE THREES:

2	3	5
4	2	3
3	1	2
3	5	1
6	3	4

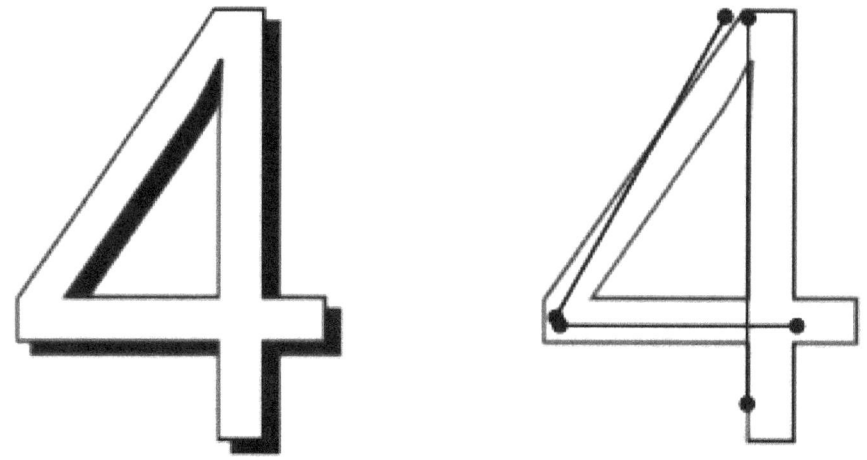

Four

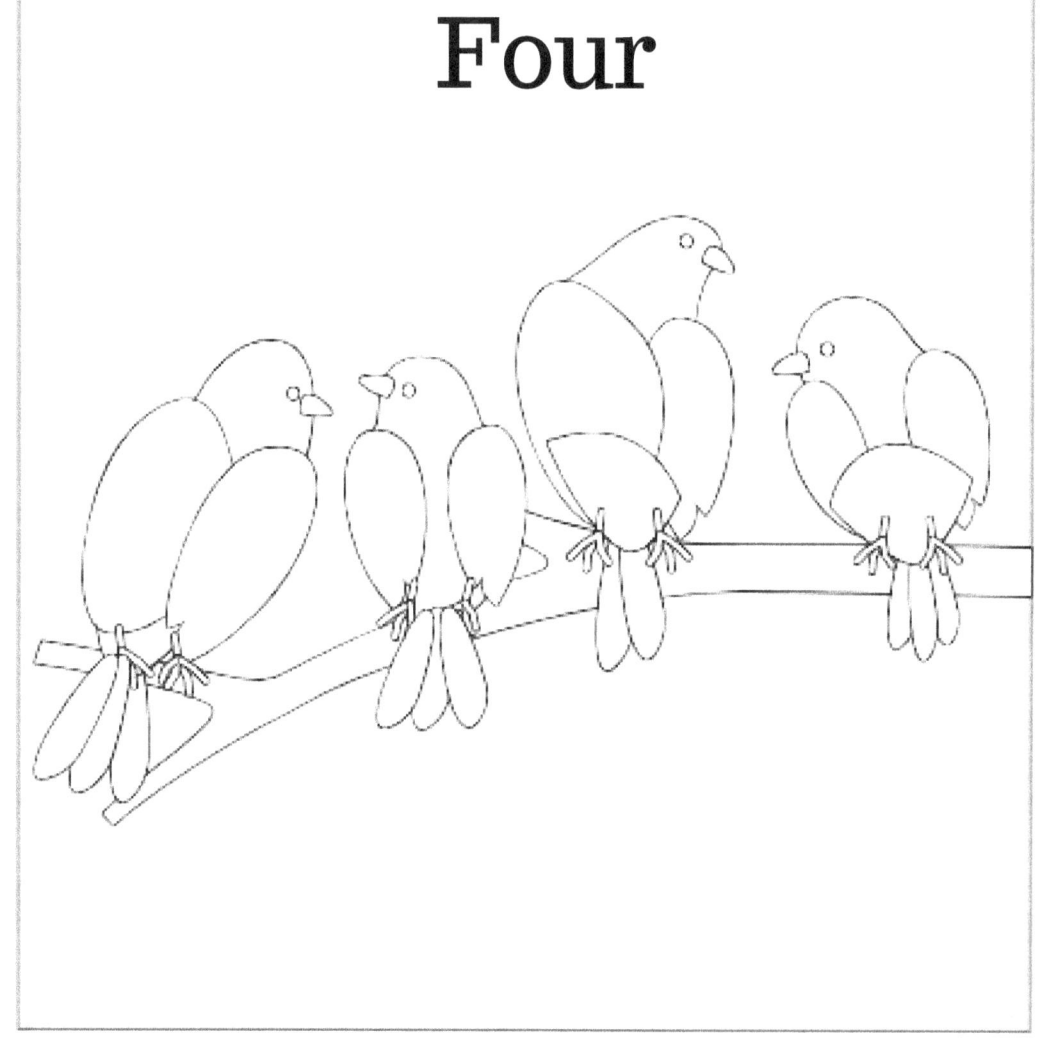

The Number Four

DIRECTIONS: TRACE THE WORDS AND NUMBERS BELOW TO PRACTICE THE NUMBER FOUR! WHEN YOU'RE FINISHED COLOR THE NUMBER.

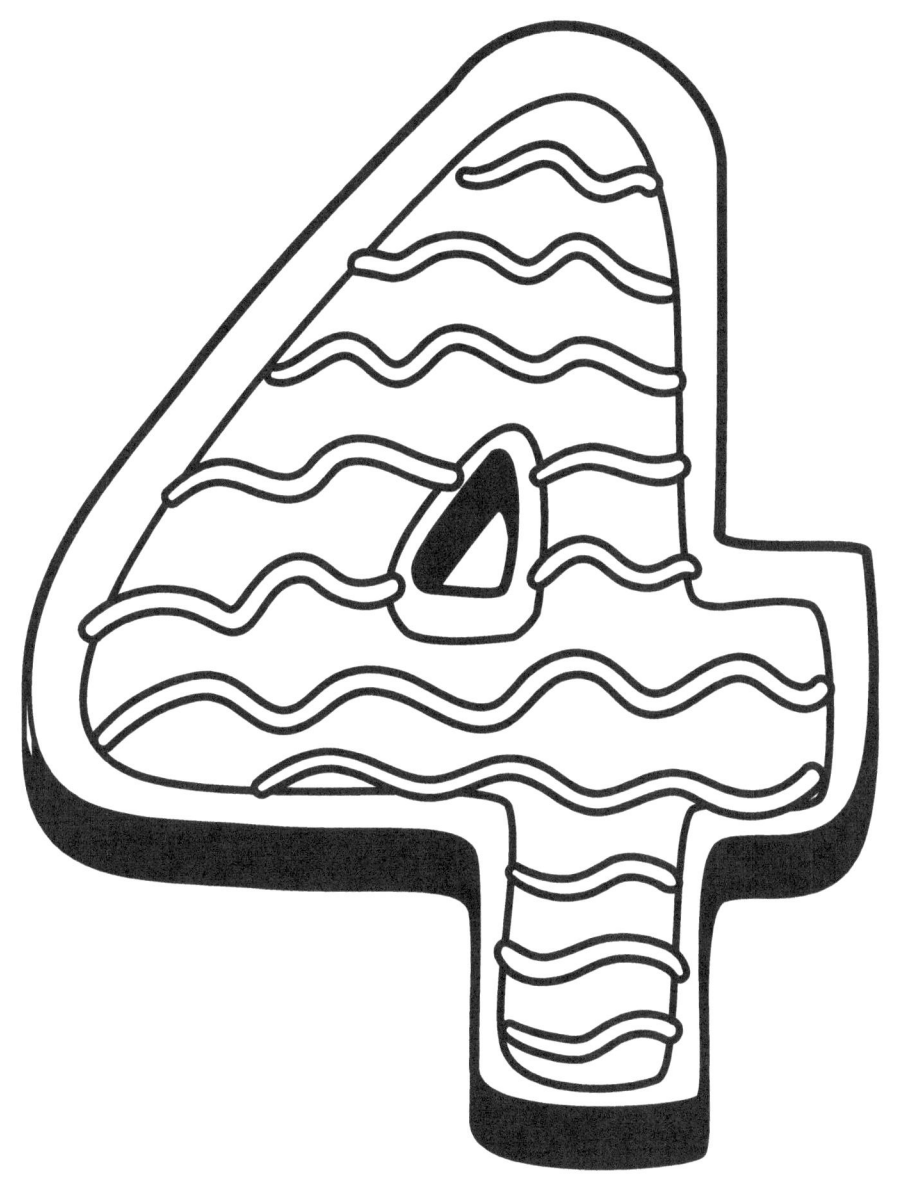

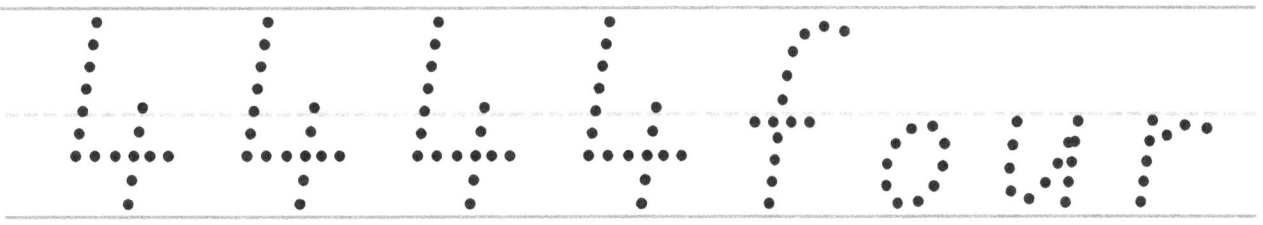

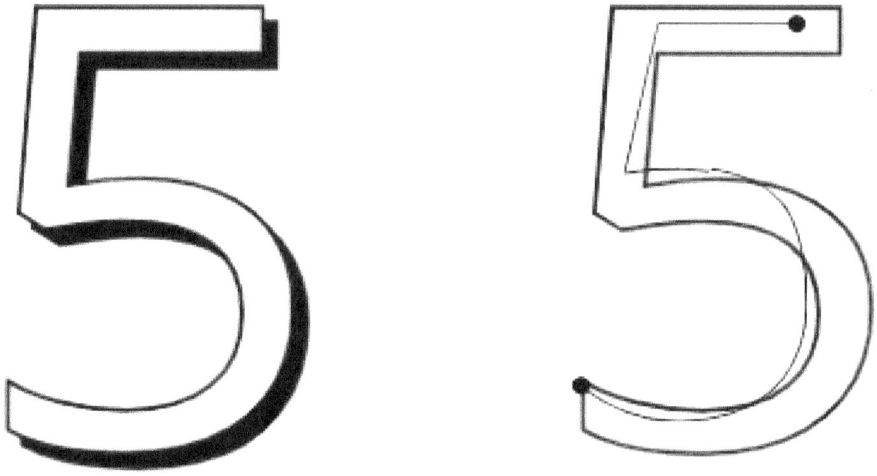

5 5

Five

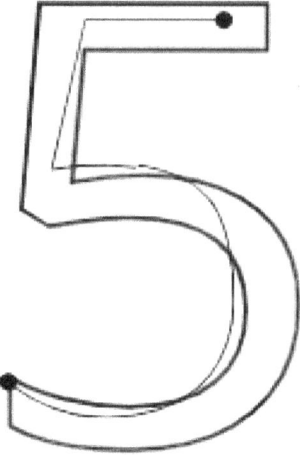

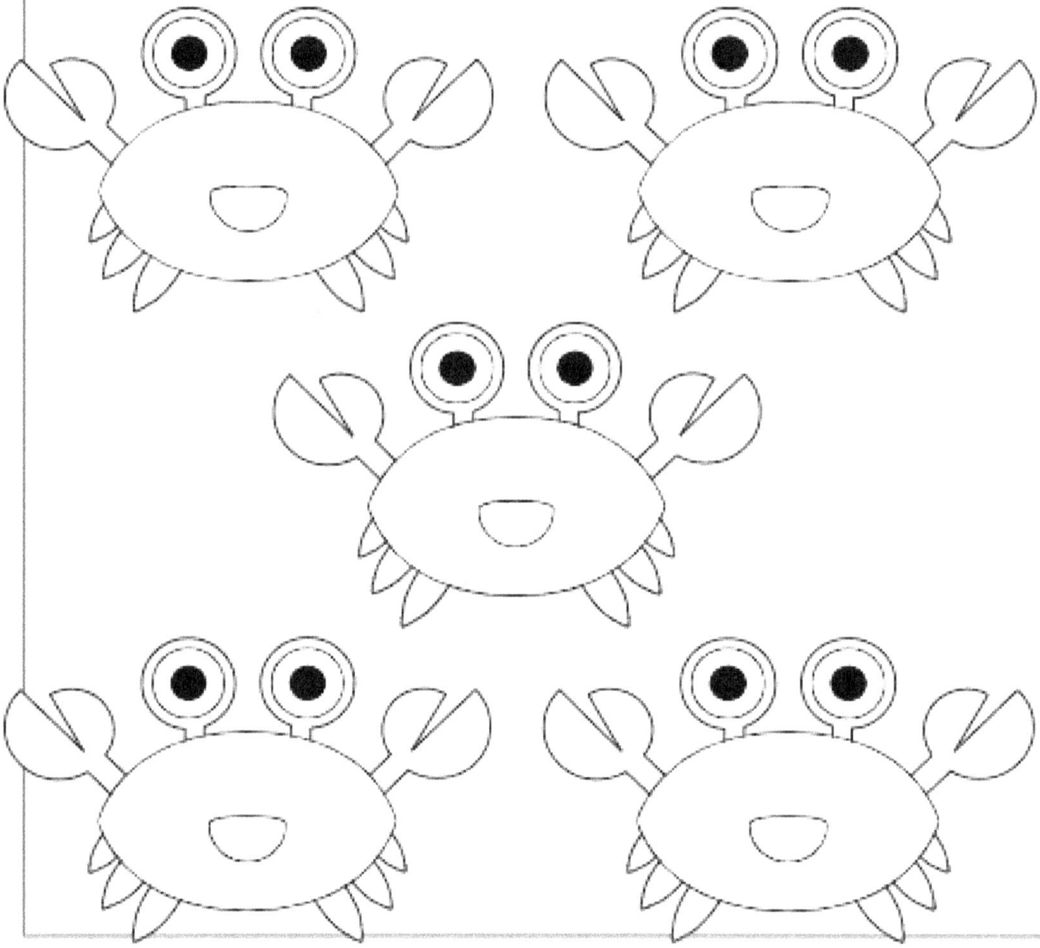

DIRECTIONS: TRACE THE WORDS AND NUMBERS BELOW.

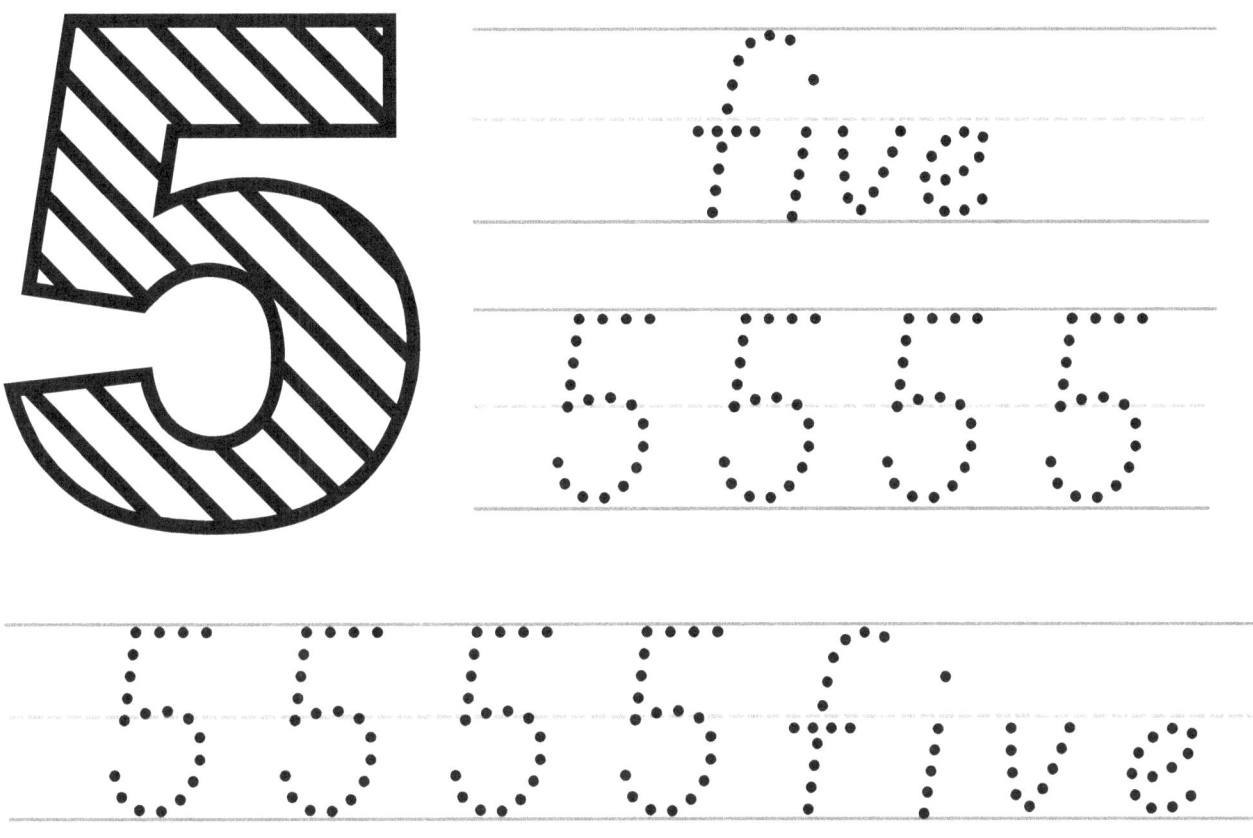

five

5 5 5 5

5 5 5 5 five

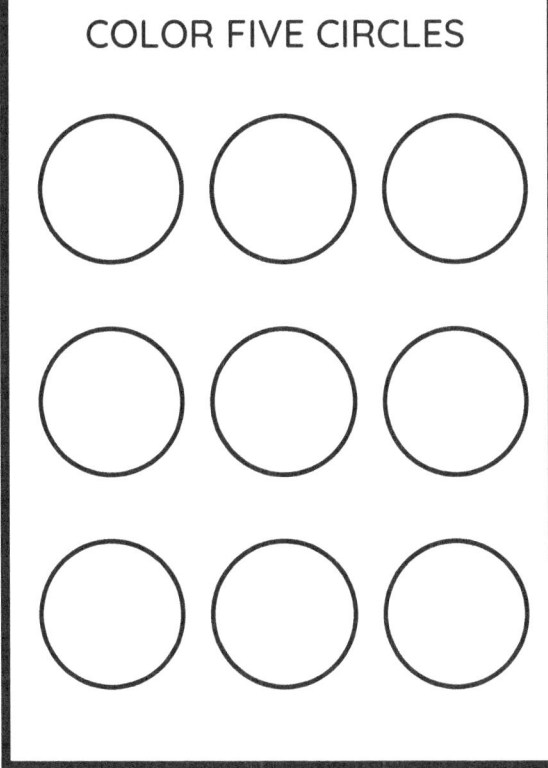

COLOR FIVE CIRCLES

CIRCLE THE FIVES

5	2	3
1	5	4
3	5	2
4	3	5
2	5	4

6 6

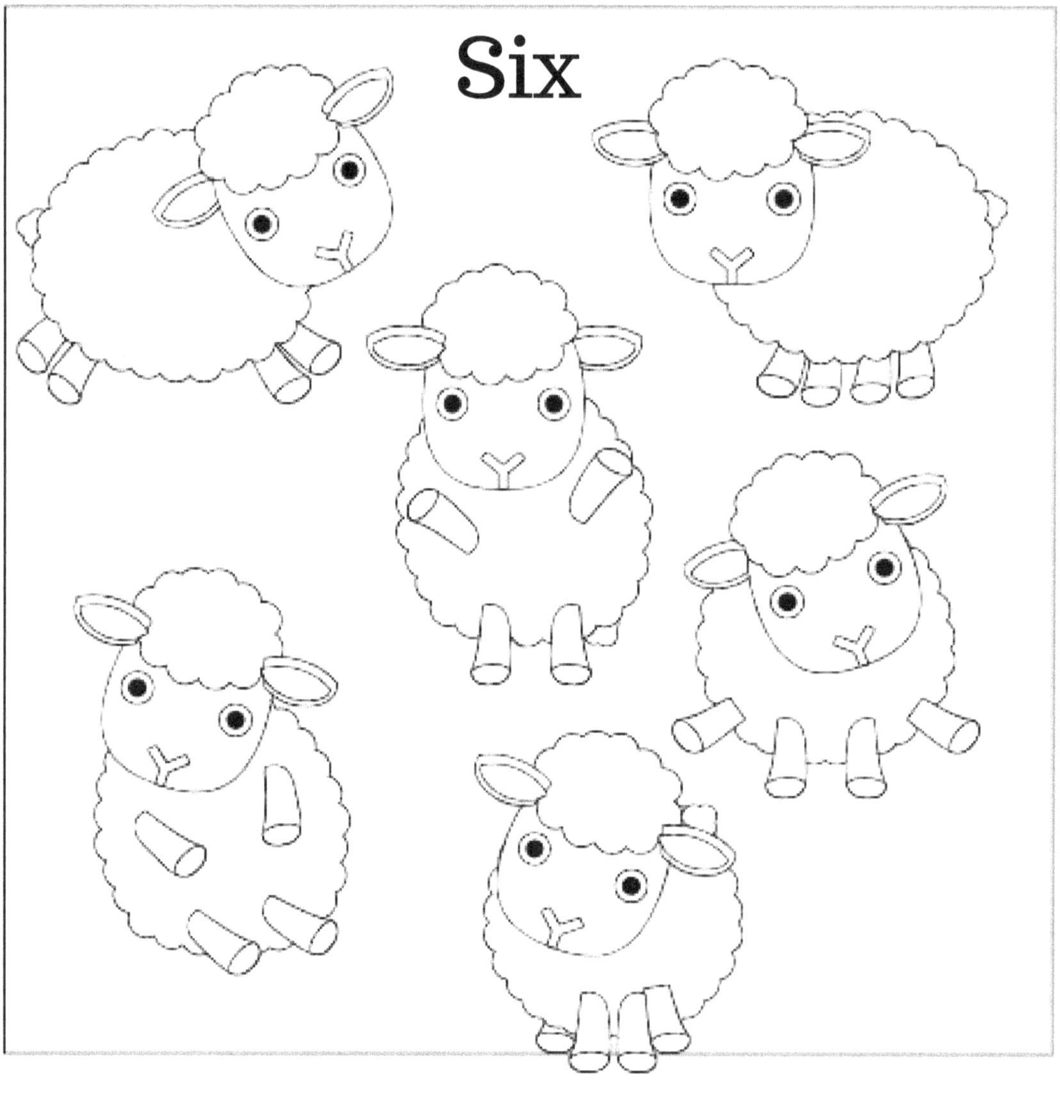

Six

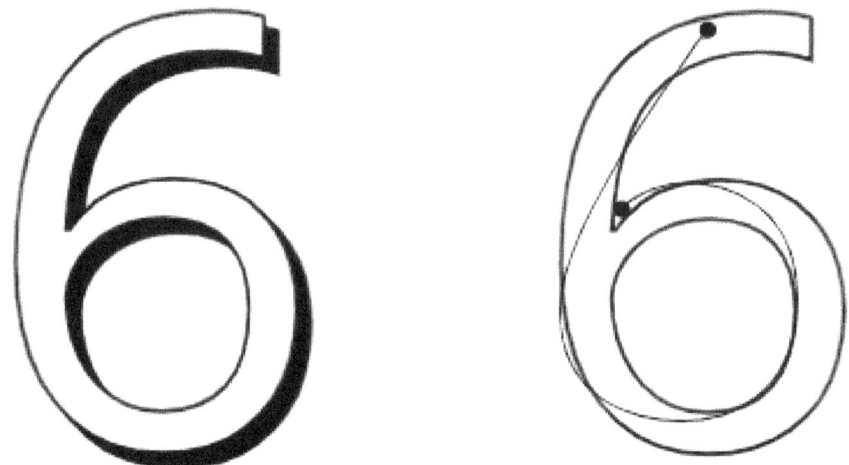

Name: _____

DIRECTIONS: TRACE THE WORDS AND NUMBERS BELOW.

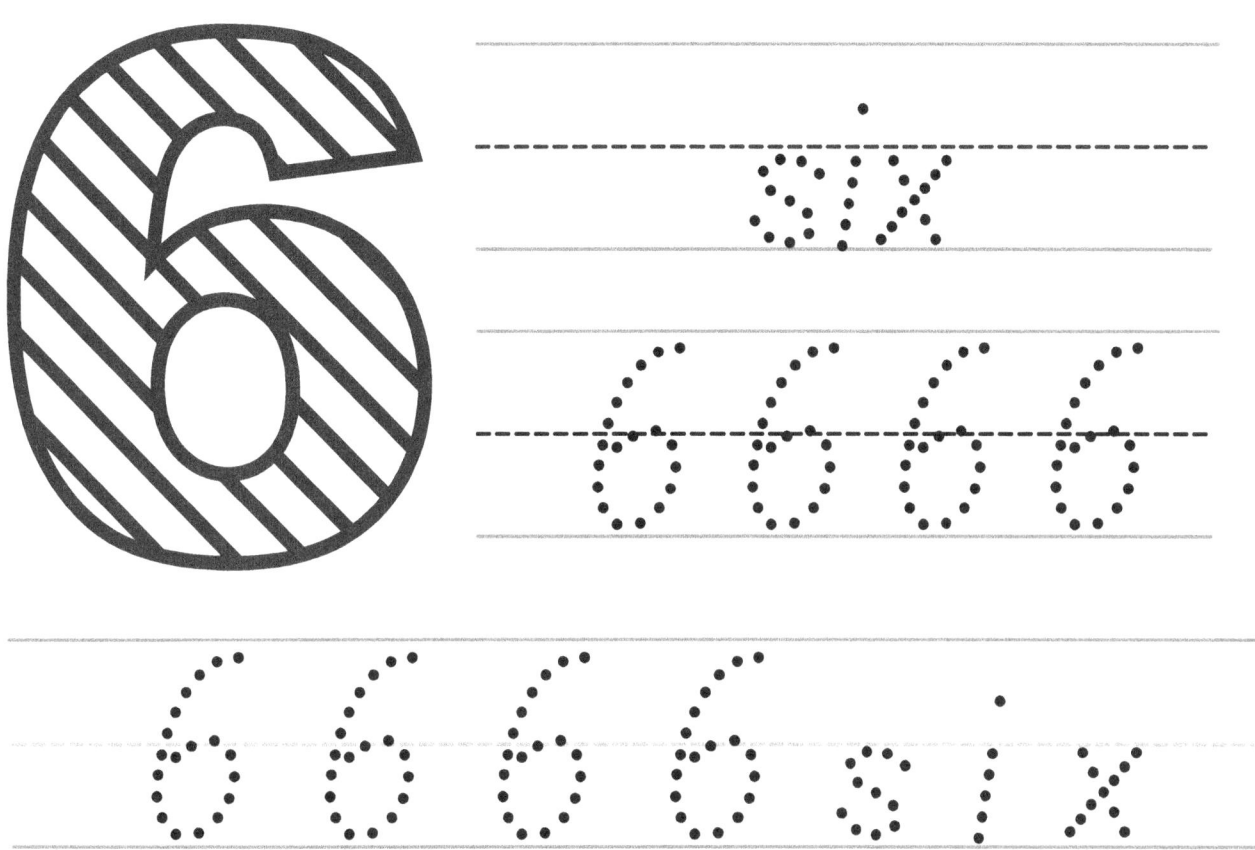

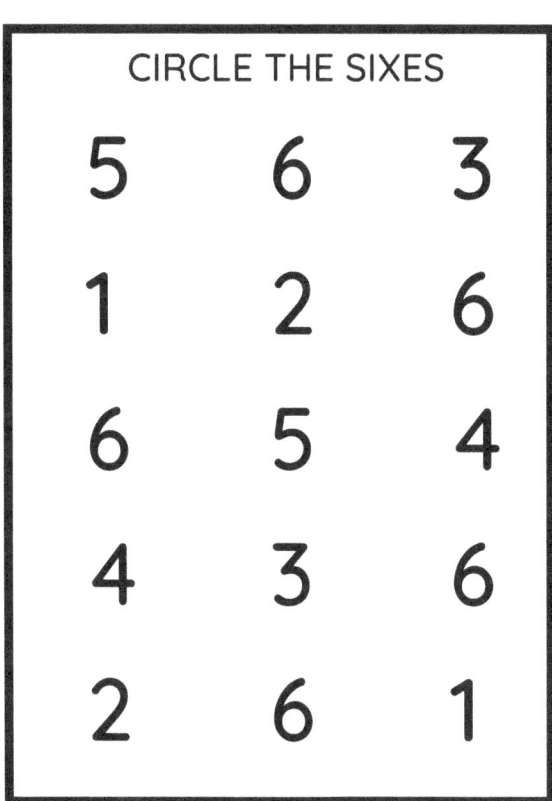

COLOR SIX TRIANGLES:

CIRCLE THE SIXES

5	6	3
1	2	6
6	5	4
4	3	6
2	6	1

7 7

Seven

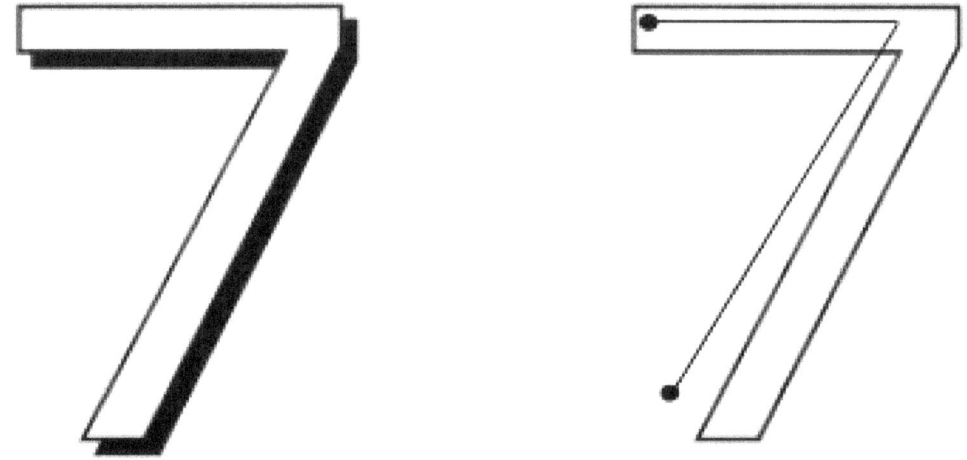

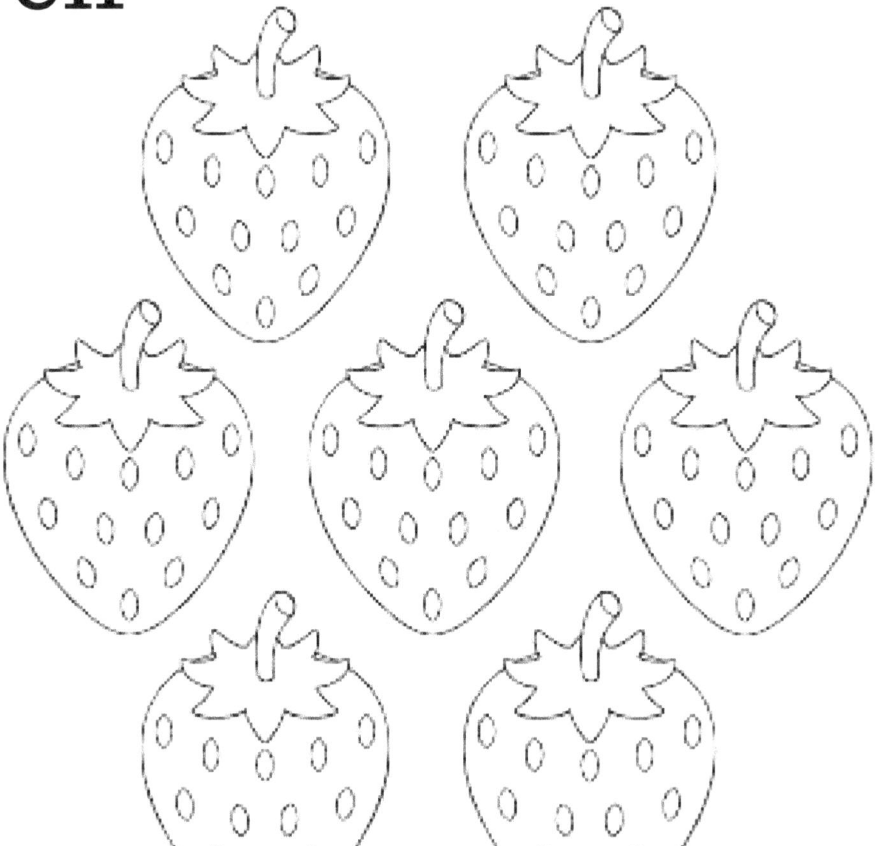

The Number Seven

DIRECTIONS: TRACE THE WORDS AND NUMBERS BELOW TO PRACTICE THE NUMBER SEVEN! WHEN YOU'RE FINISHED COLOR THE NUMBER.

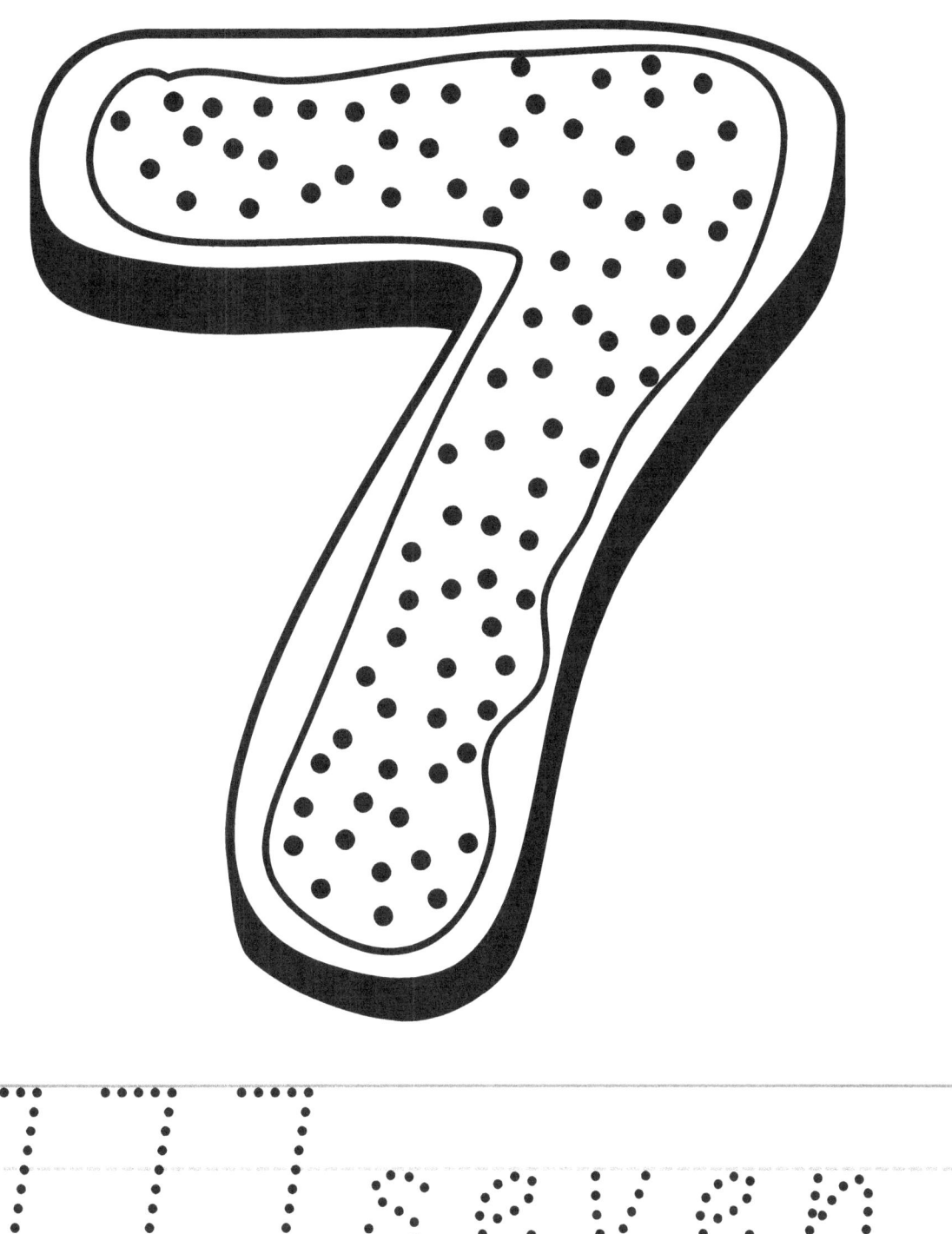

7 7 7 seven

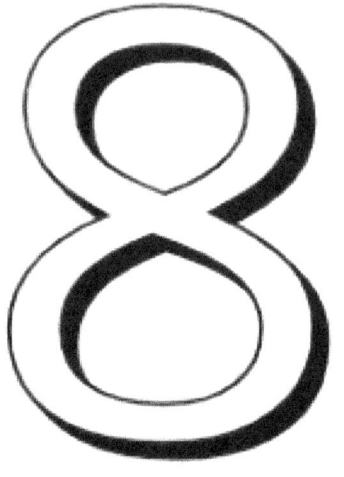 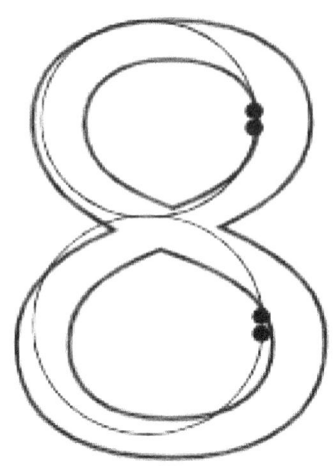

Eight

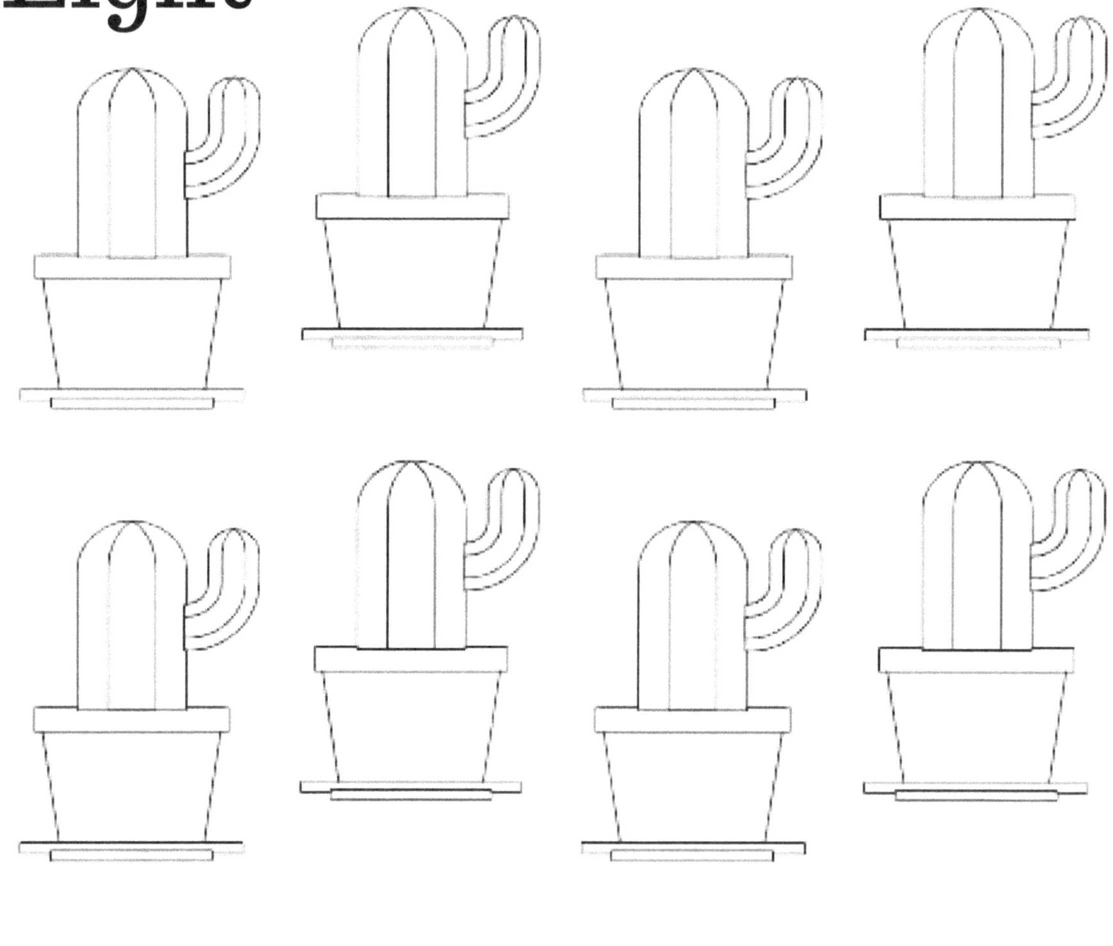

DIRECTIONS: TRACE THE WORDS AND NUMBERS BELOW.

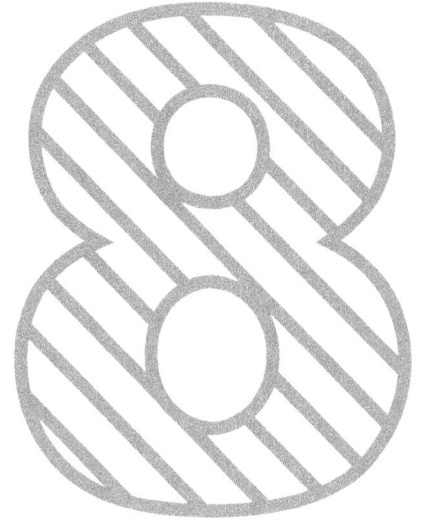

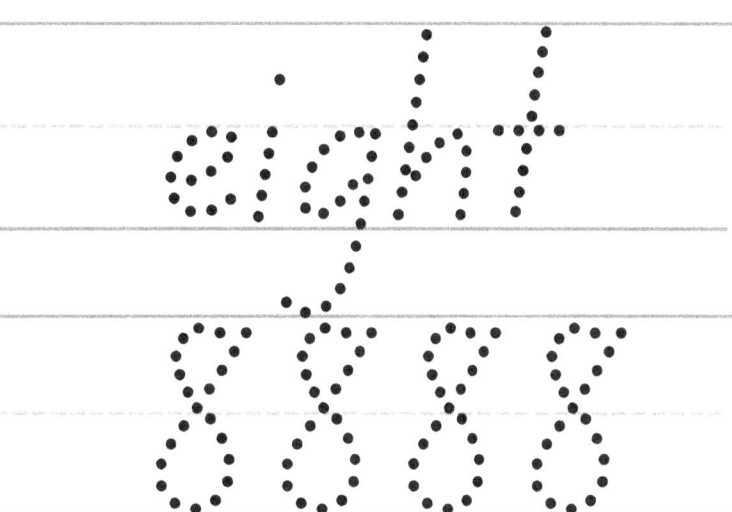

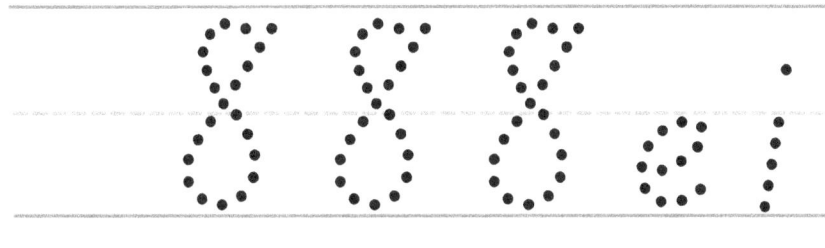

COLOR EIGHT DIAMONDS:

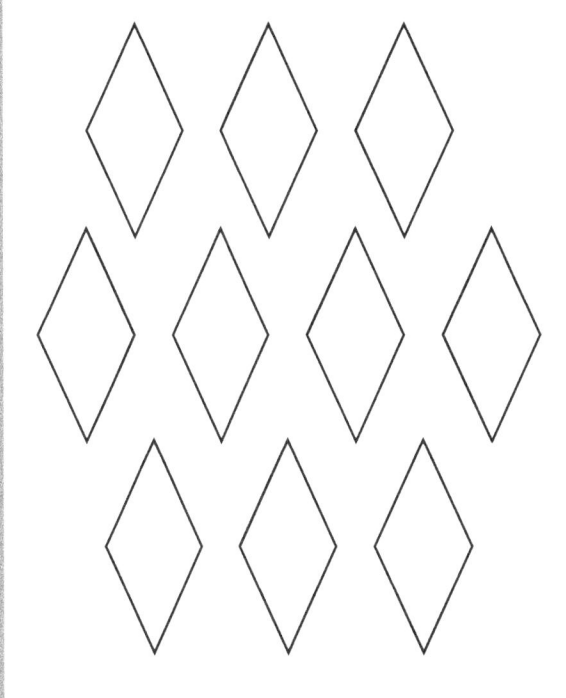

CIRCLE THE EIGHTS:

1	8	3
4	5	8
8	6	2
4	3	8
2	5	1

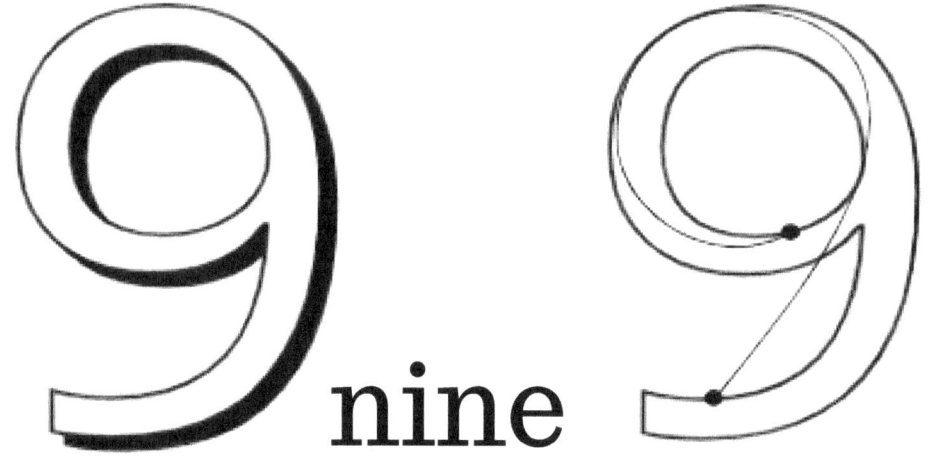

9 nine 9

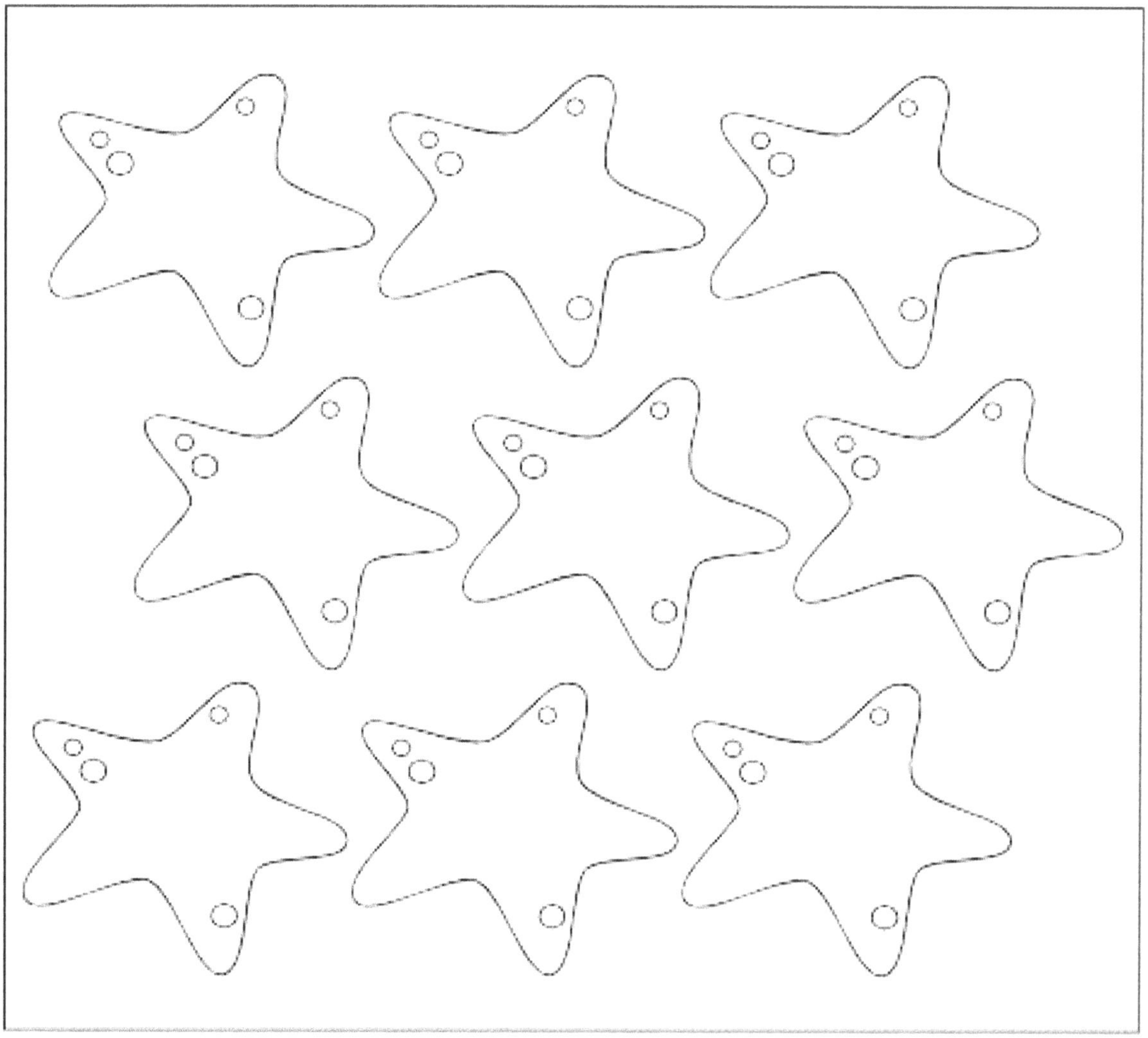

The Number Nine

DIRECTIONS: TRACE THE WORDS AND NUMBERS BELOW TO PRACTICE THE NUMBER NINE! WHEN YOU'RE FINISHED COLOR THE NUMBER.

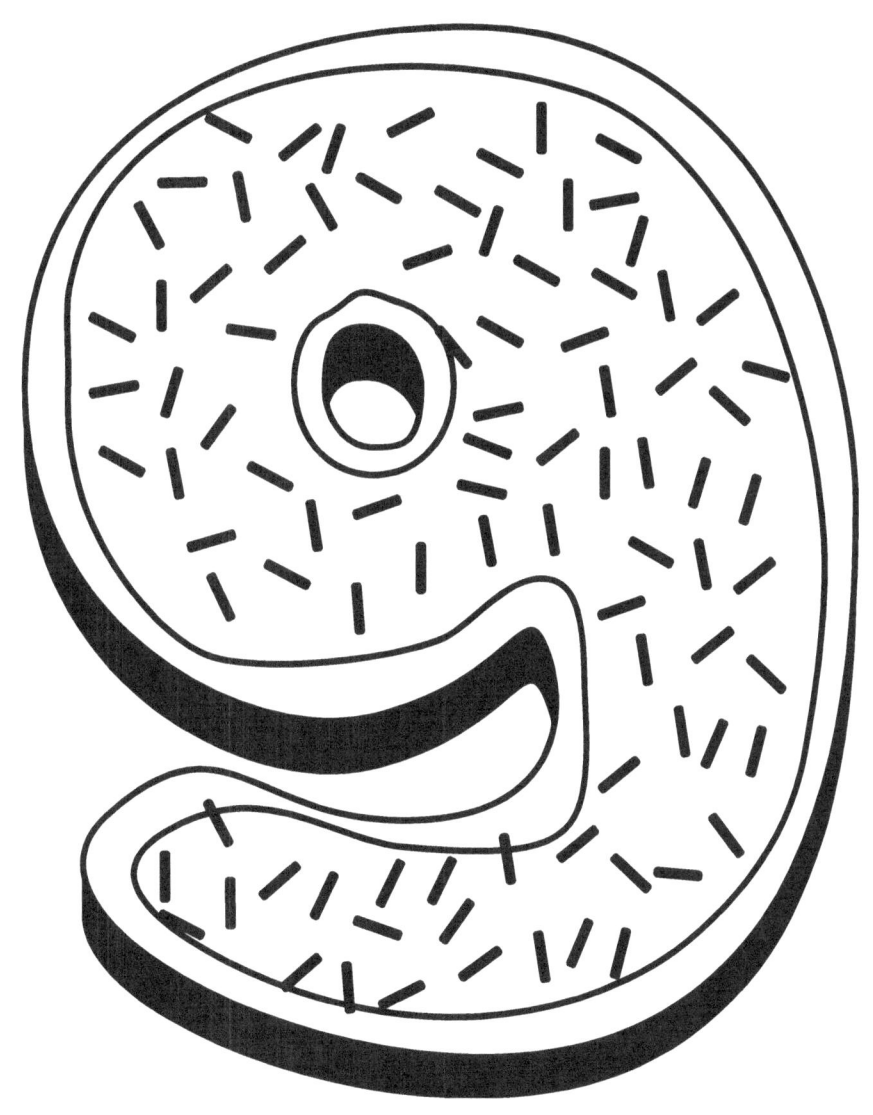

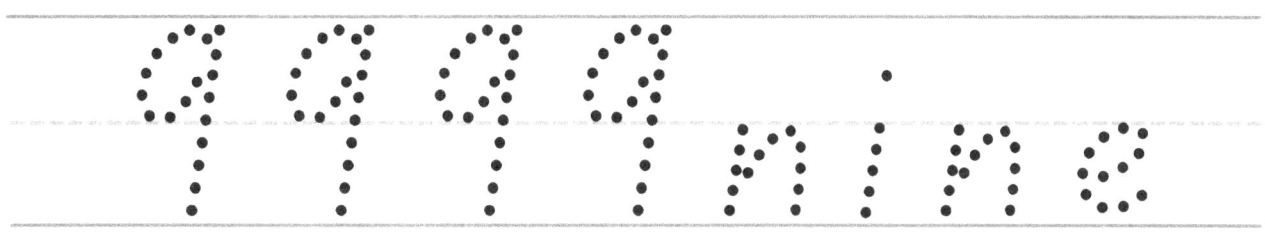

10 10

Ten

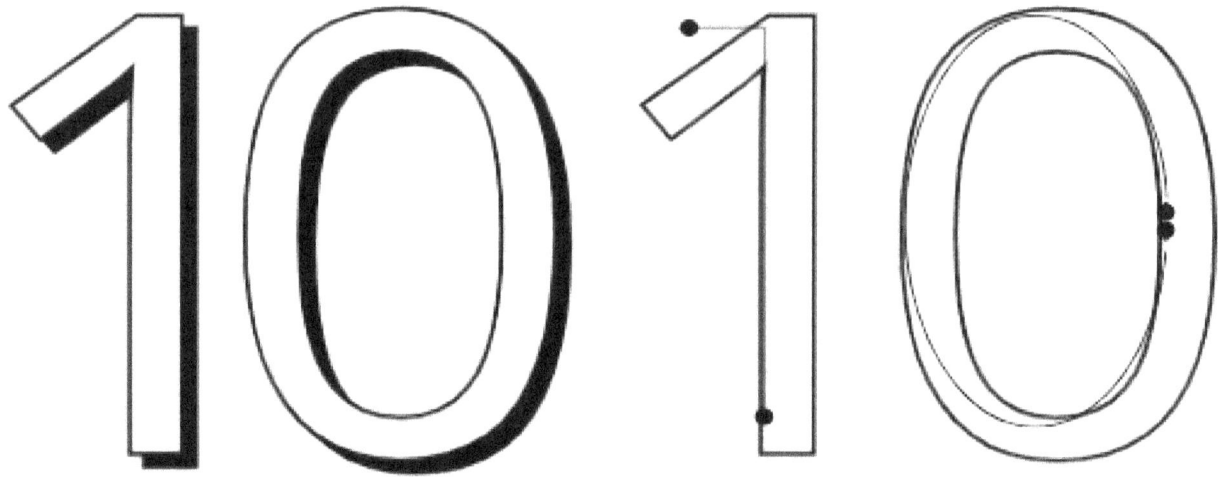

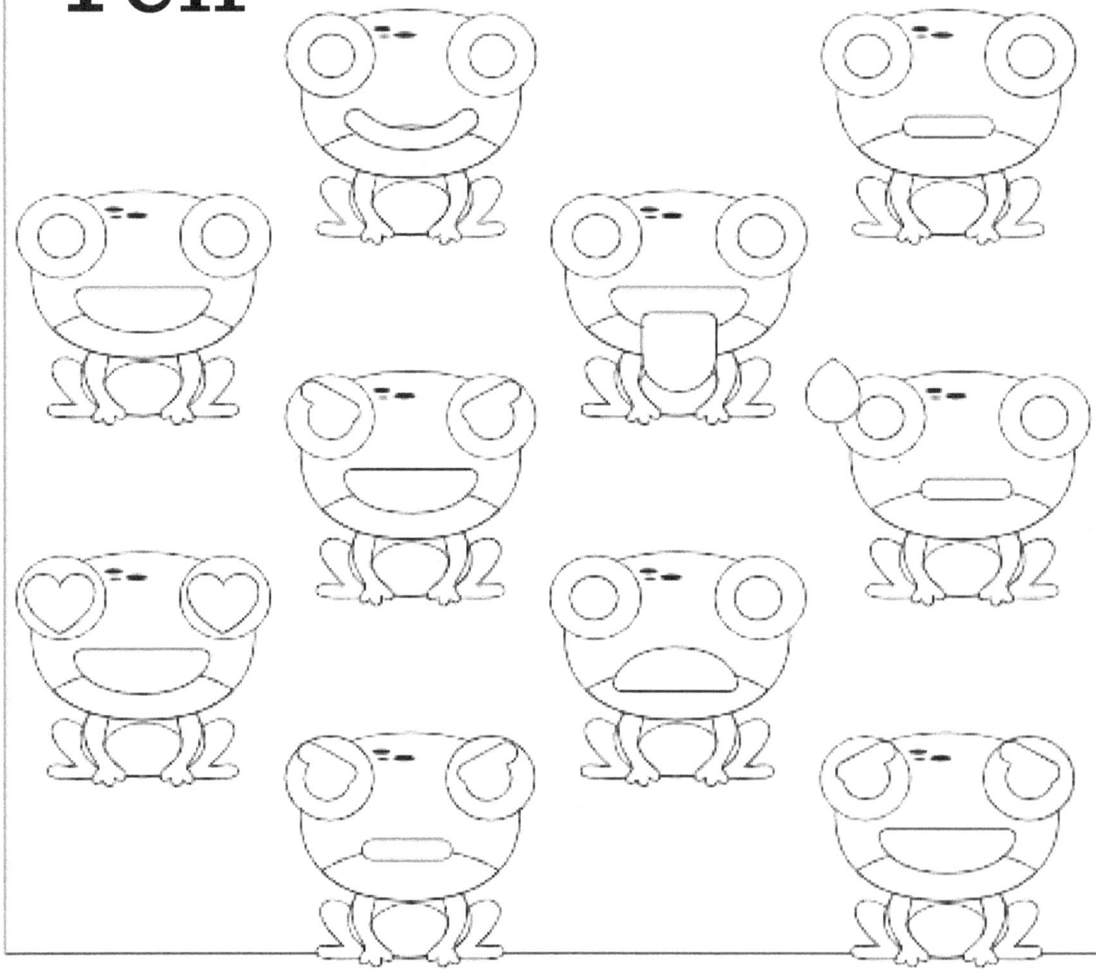

Name: _____

The Number Ten

DIRECTIONS: TRACE THE WORDS AND NUMBERS BELOW TO PRACTICE THE NUMBER TEN! WHEN YOU'RE FINISHED COLOR THE NUMBER.

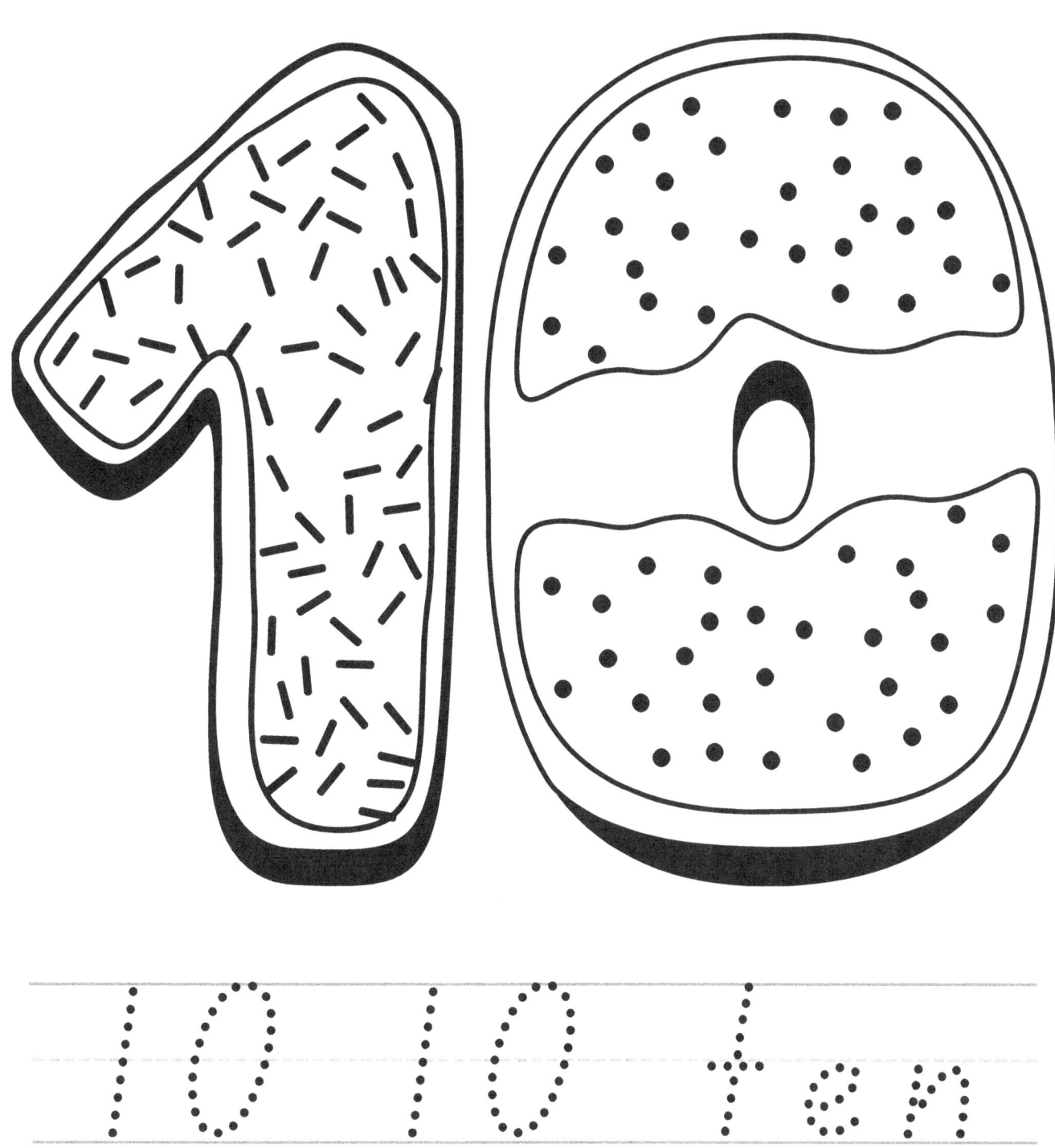

10   10   ten

Roll 'em and Add 'em

Add up the dice pictured. Put the answer in the space provided.
Turn the page over and use your own dice to roll numbers for
the equation.

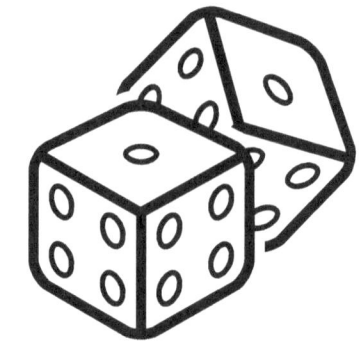

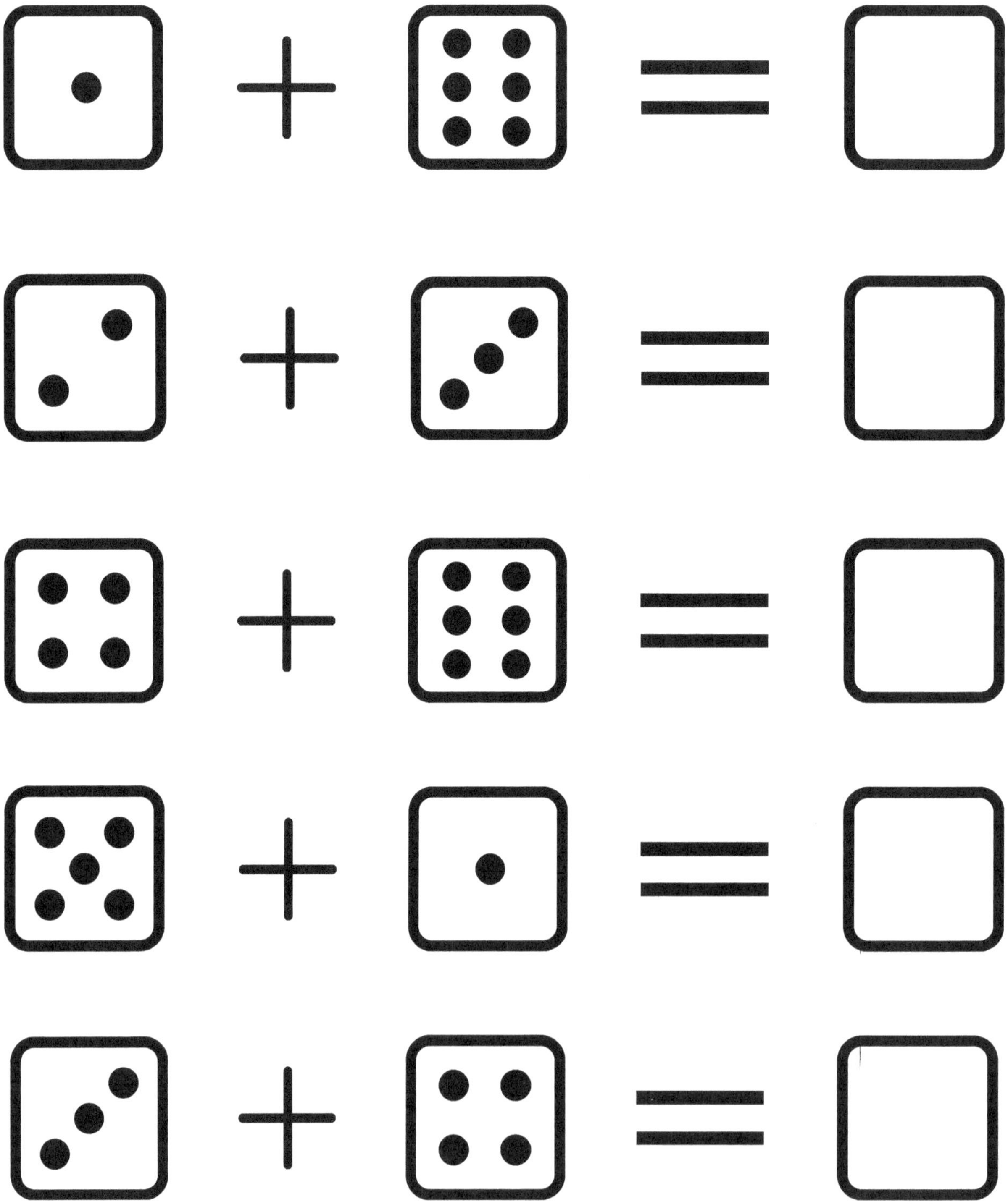

$1 + 6 = \boxed{}$

$2 + 3 = \boxed{}$

$4 + 6 = \boxed{}$

$5 + 1 = \boxed{}$

$3 + 4 = \boxed{}$

DIRECTIONS: COLOR THE PICTURE USING THE SOLUTION TO THE MATH
QUESTION TO SELECT THE COLOR!

1 = Brown
2 = Black
3 = Orange
4 = Pink
5 = Red

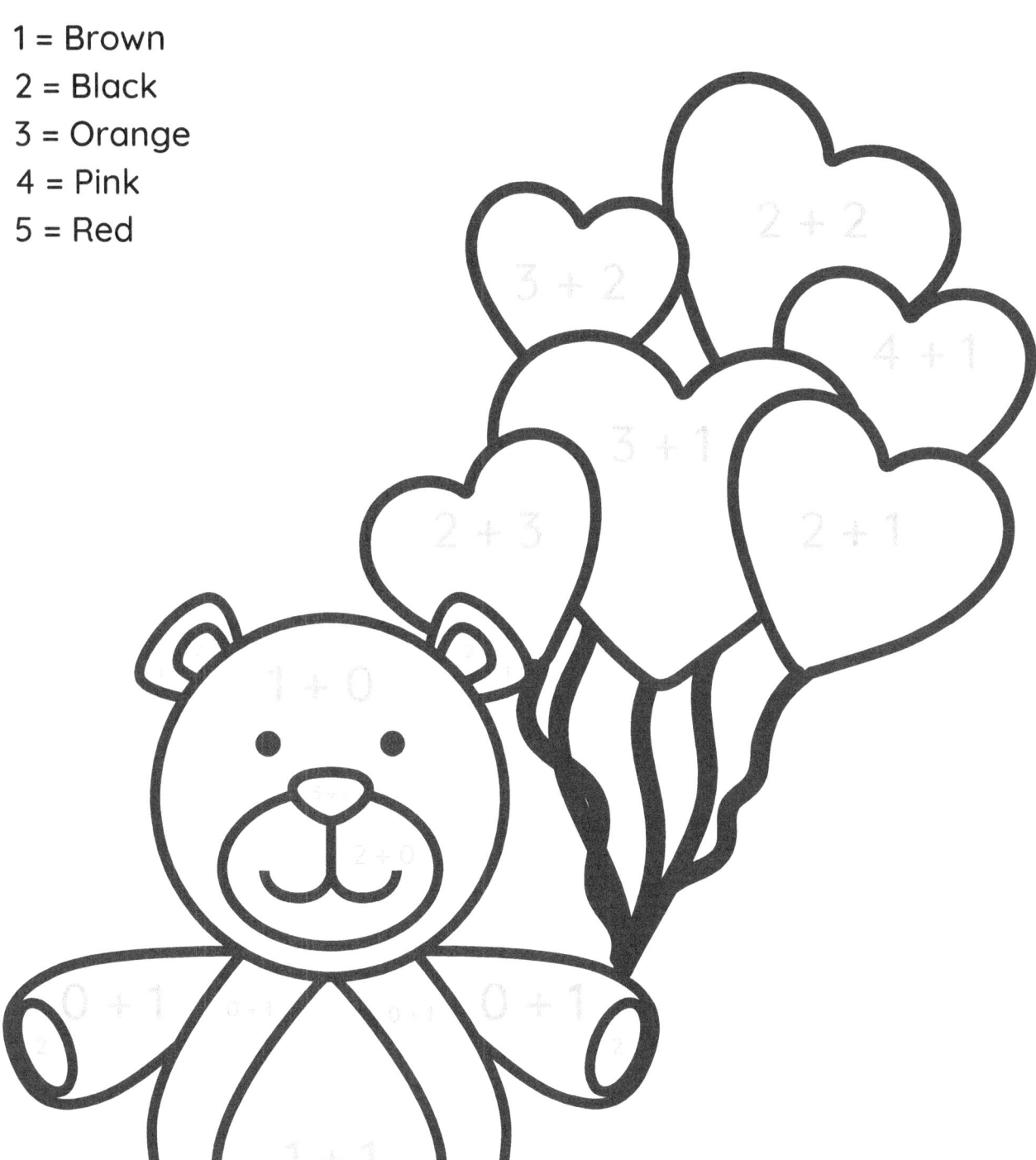

Number Values

Color the number that has the bigger value

5 8	4 5
6 0	3 2
9 5	4 7
8 2	6 1

LADYBUG NUMBERS

Trace the numbers 1-12 on the ladybugs below.
When you are finished, color the ladybugs' wings
using red and black.

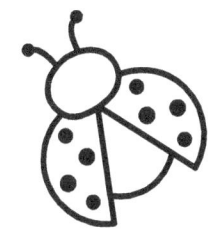

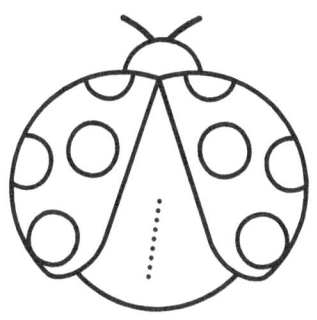 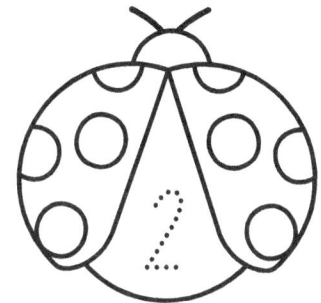 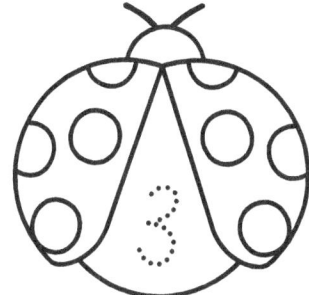

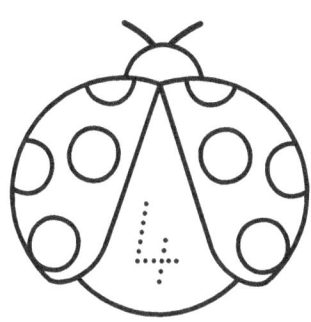 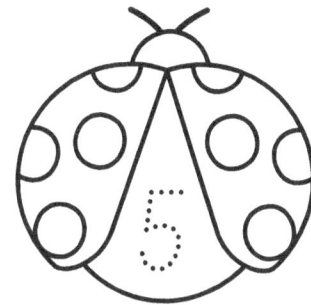 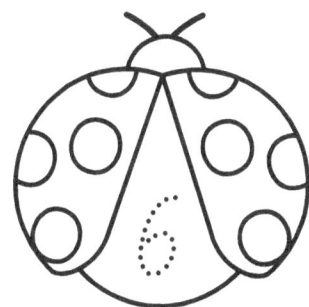

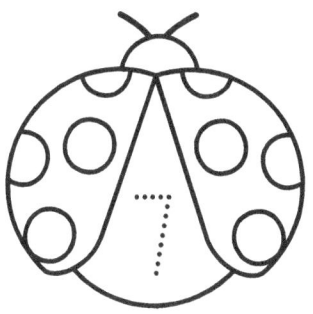 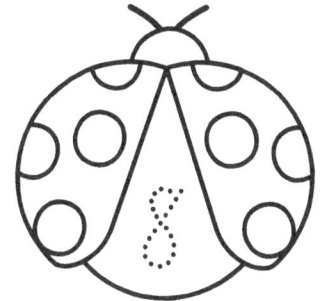 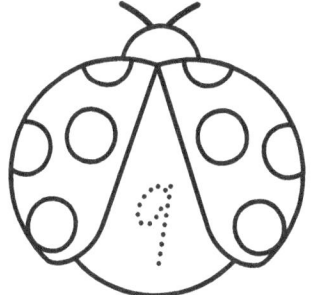

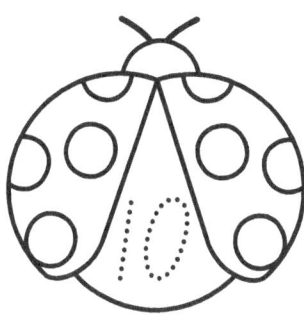 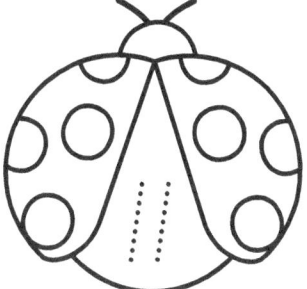 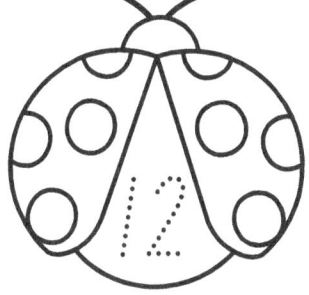

Aa

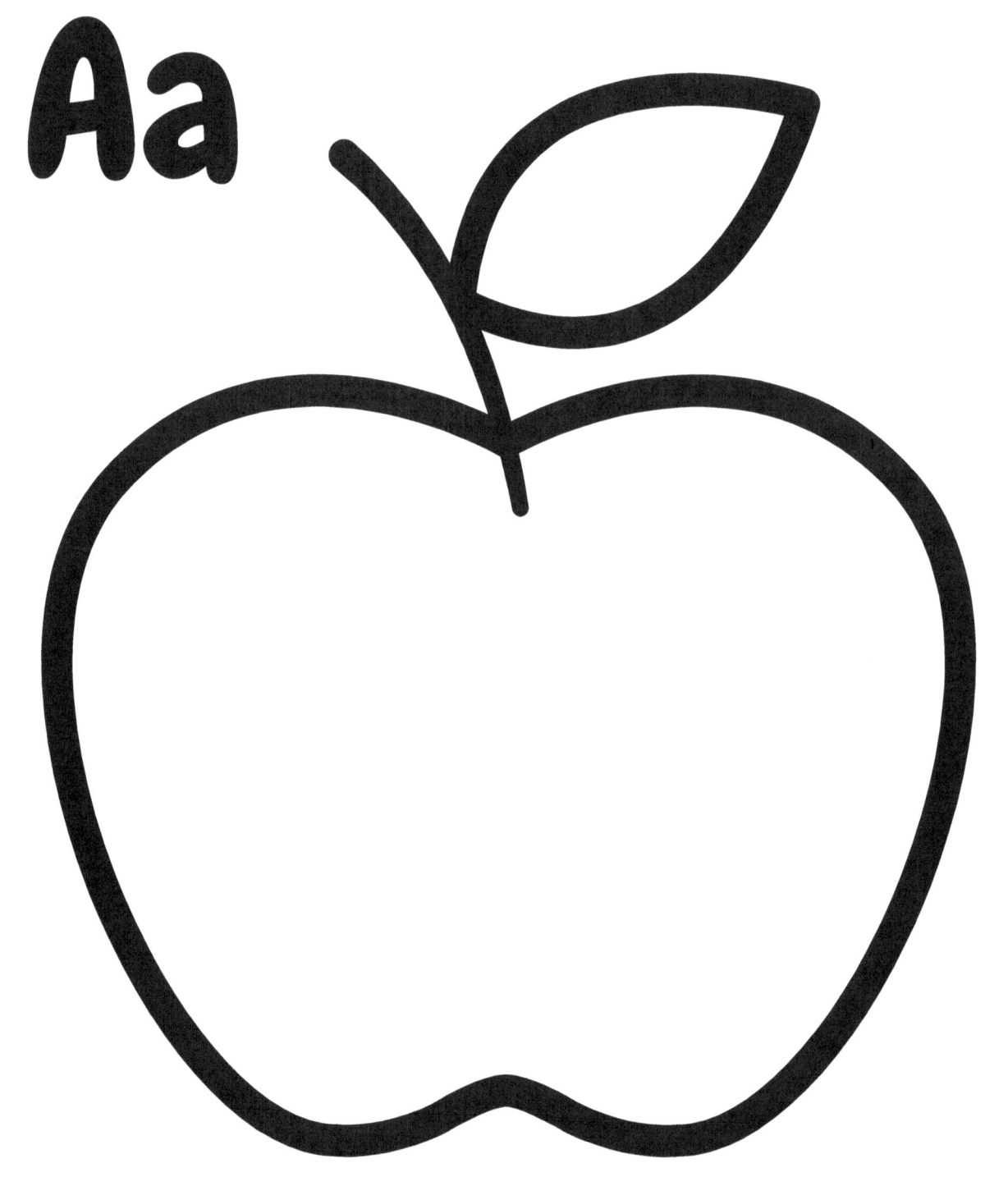

apple

Bb

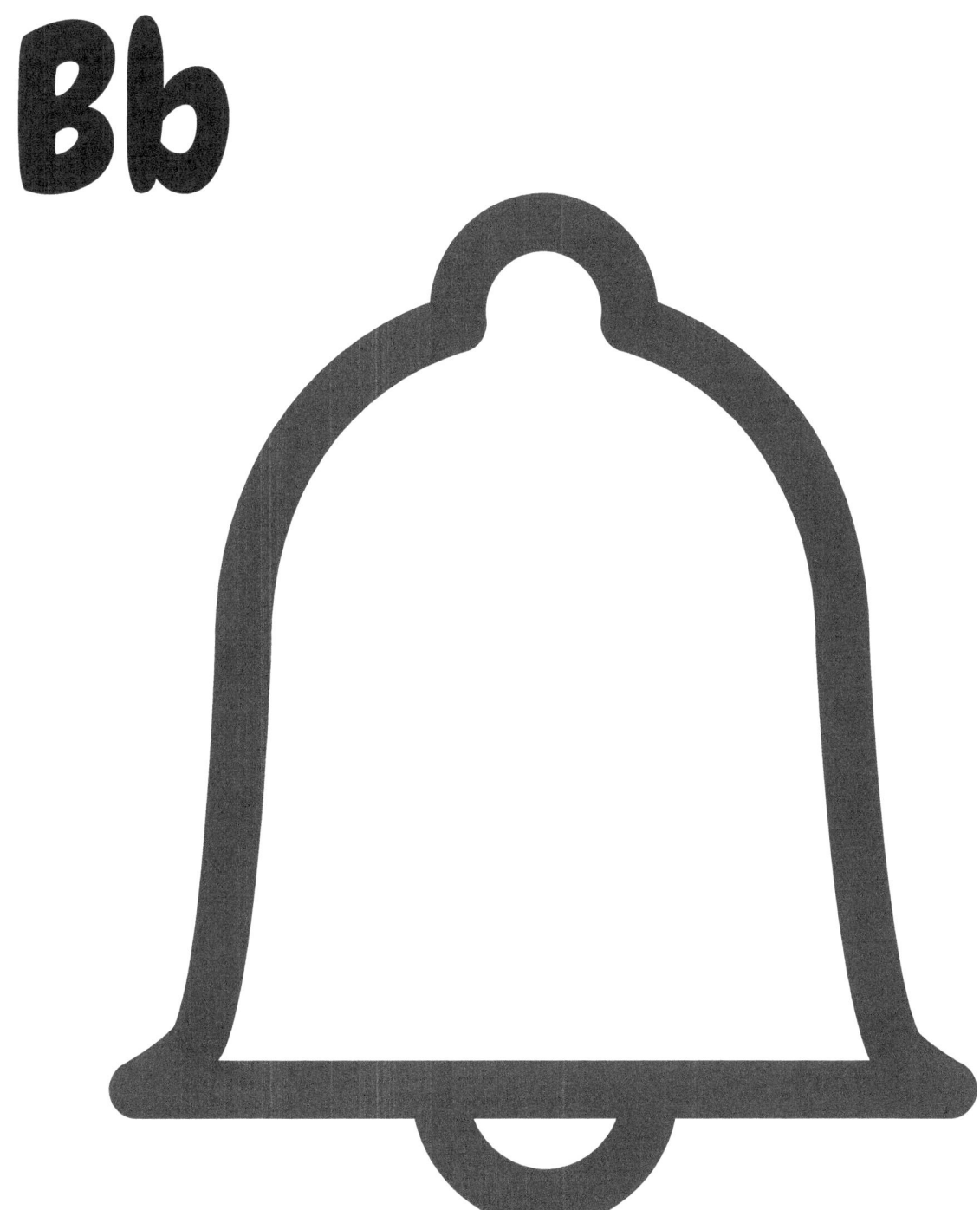

bell

Cc

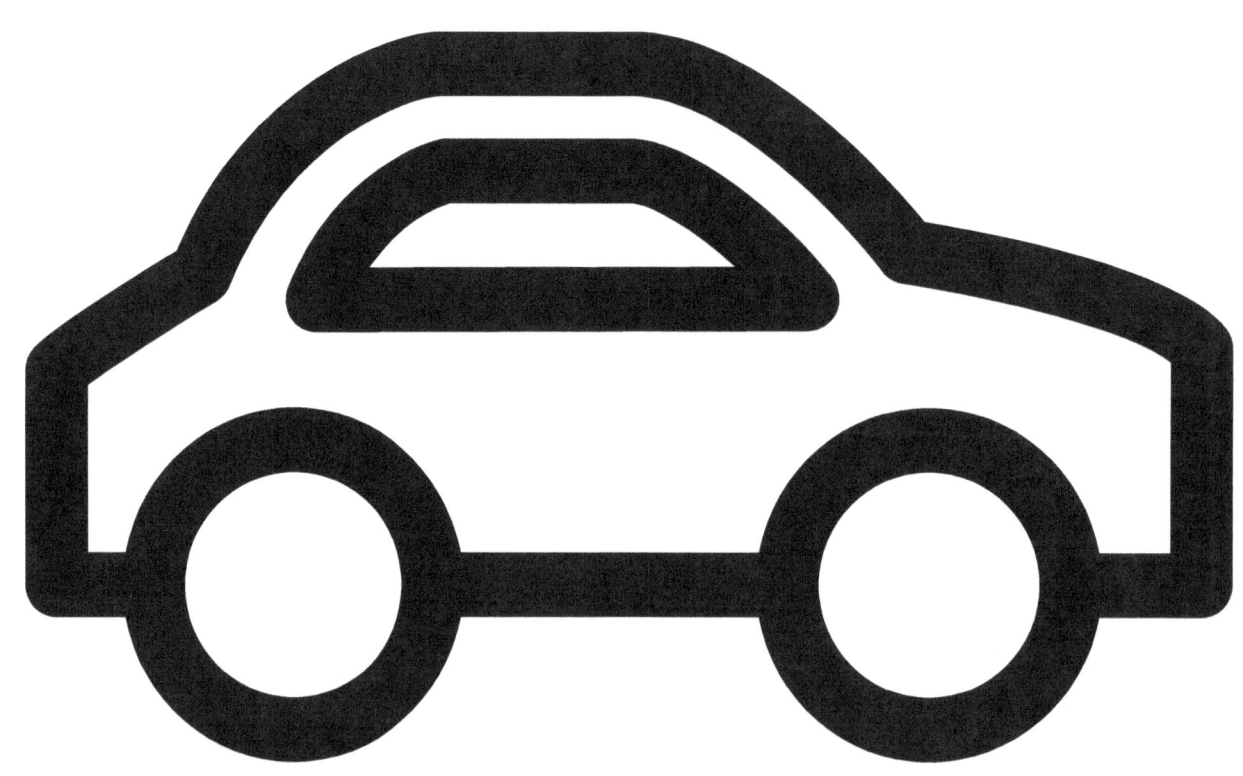

car

Dd

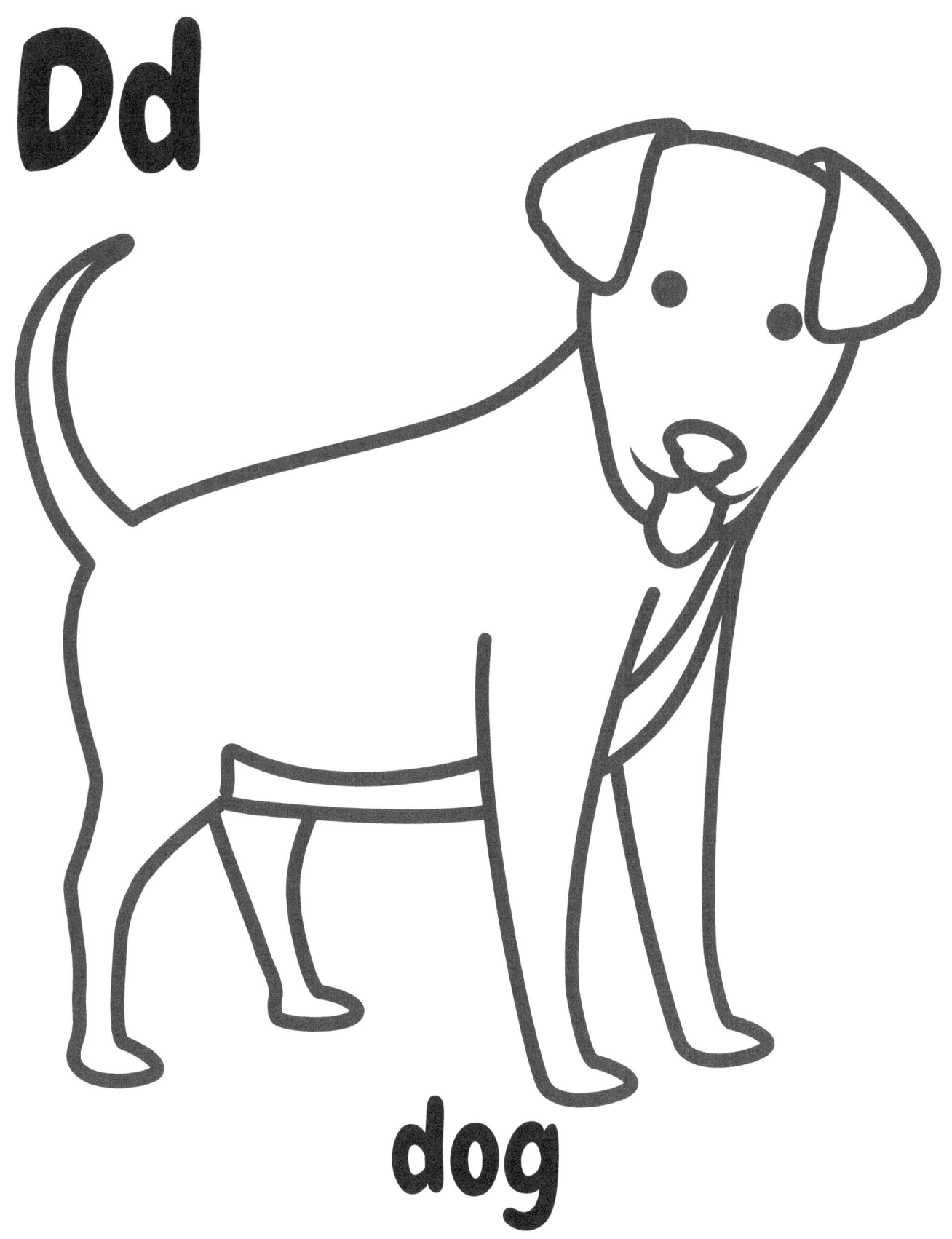

dog

Ee

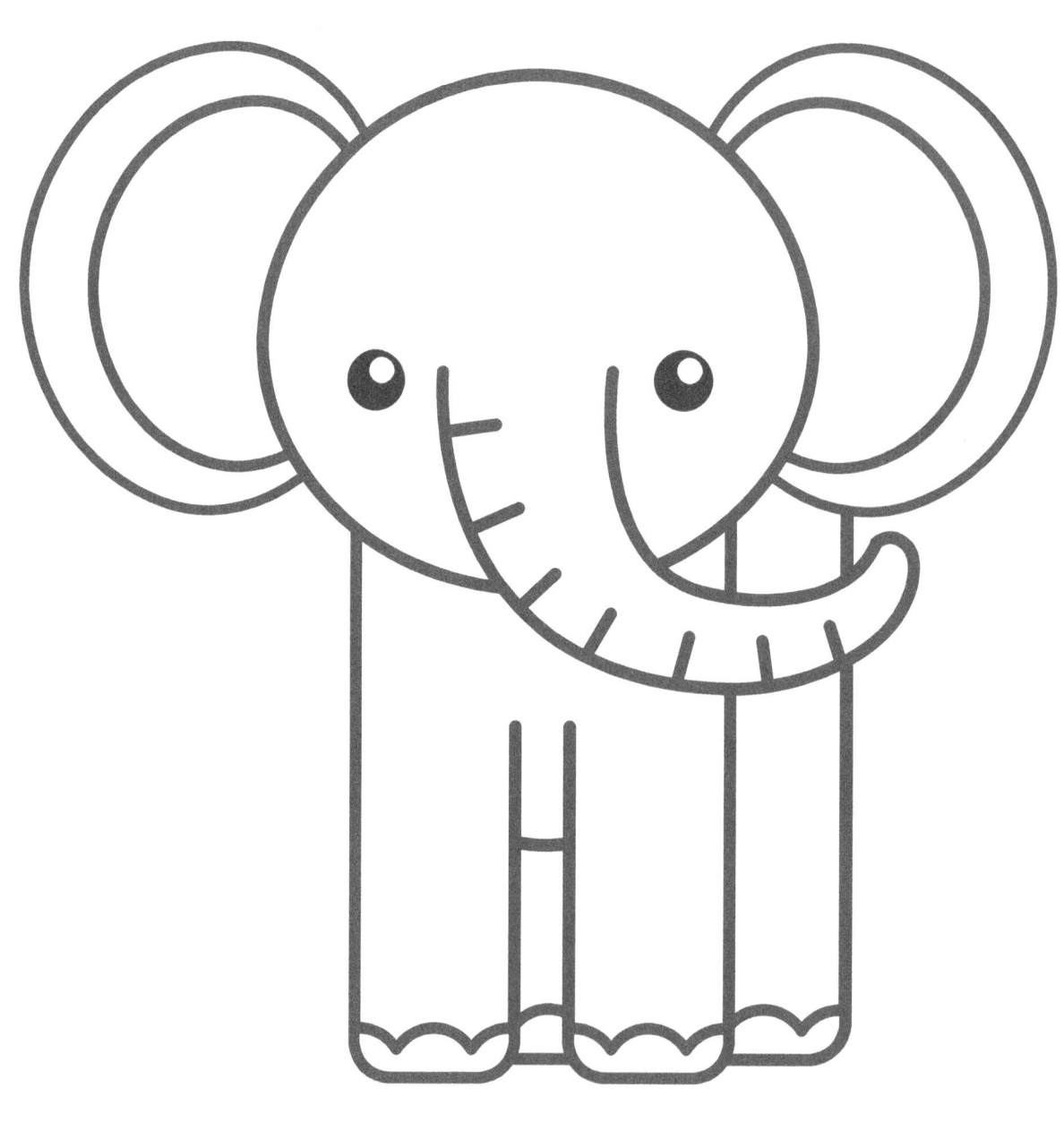

elephant

Ff

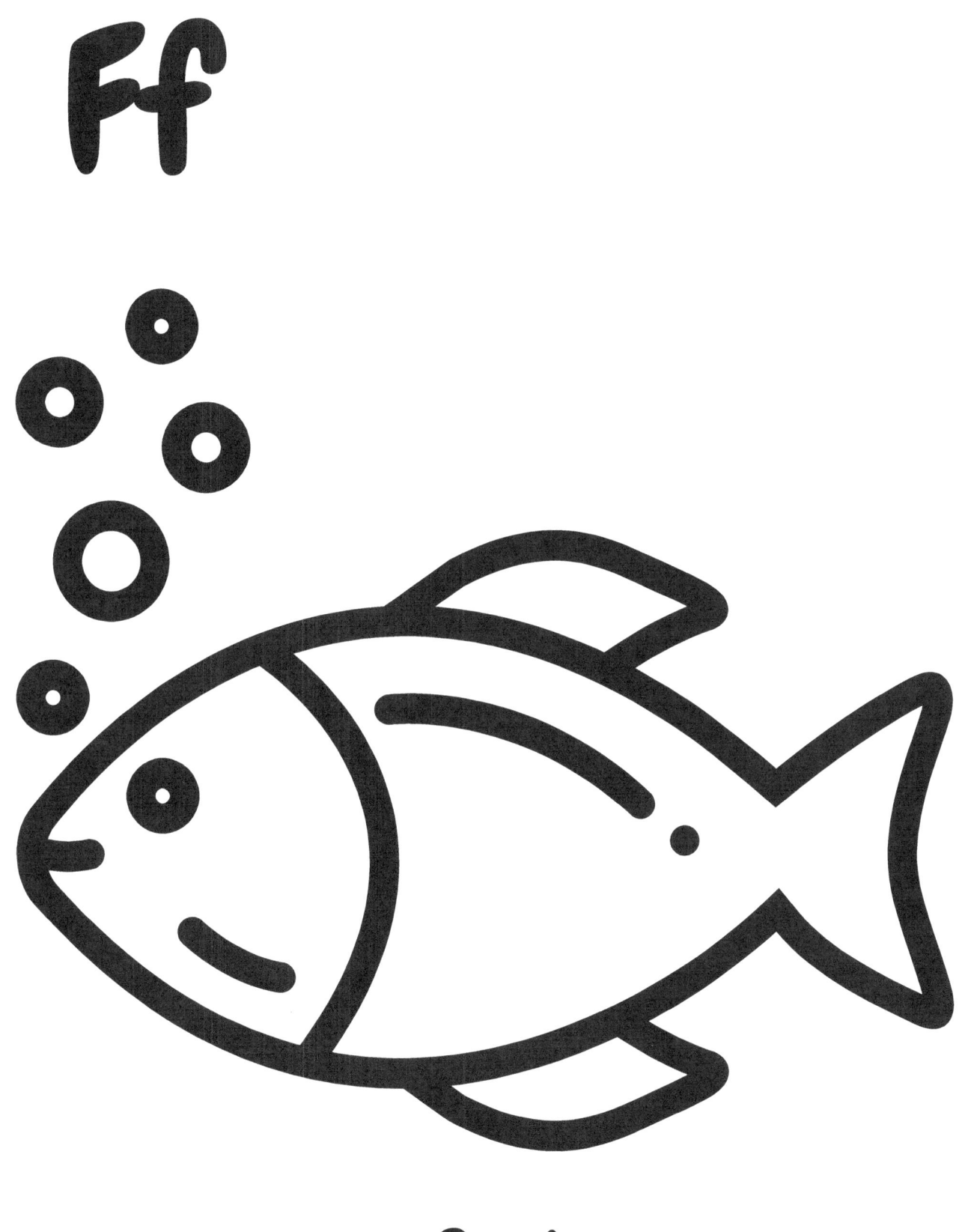

fish

Gg

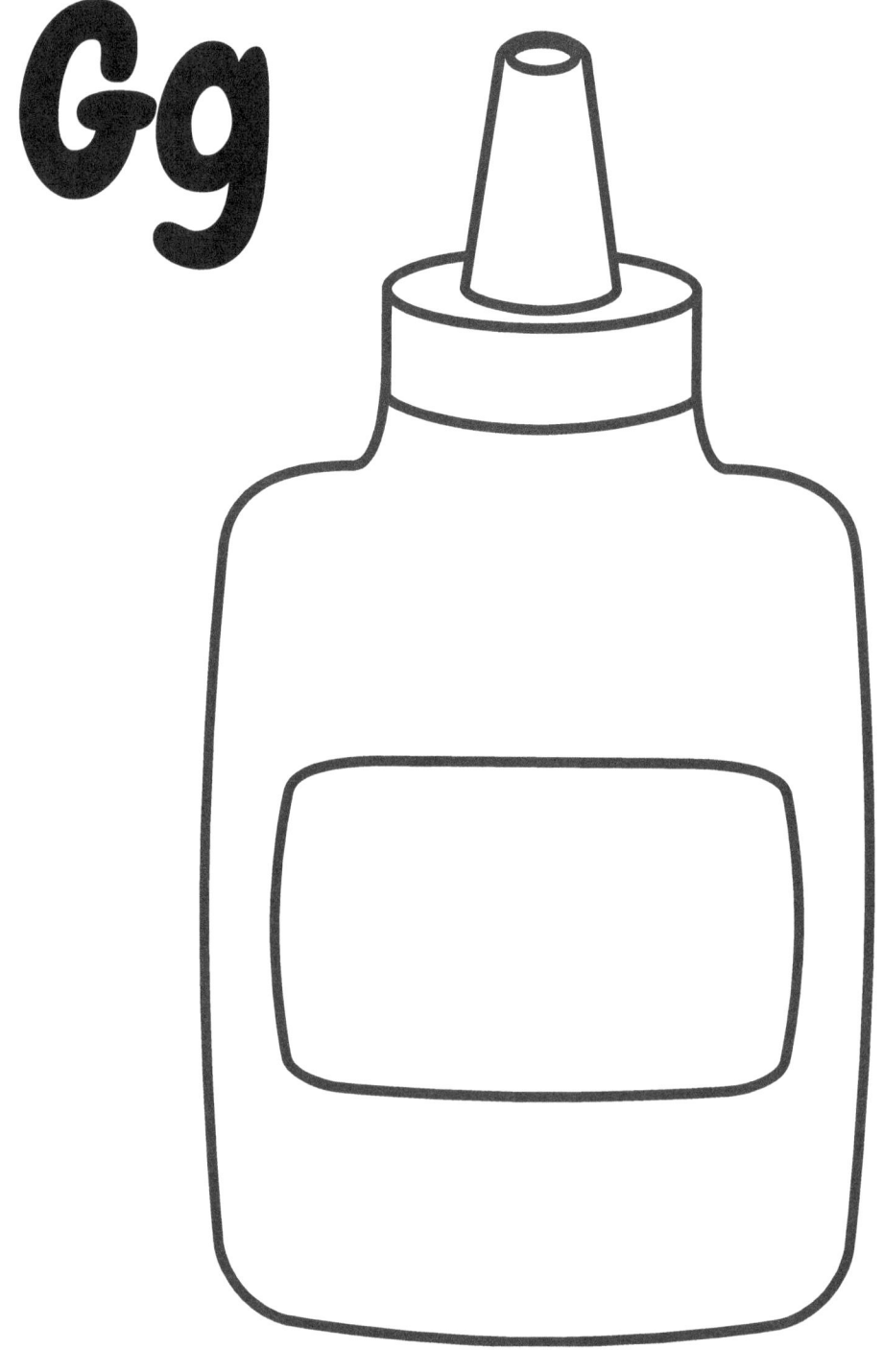

glue

Hh

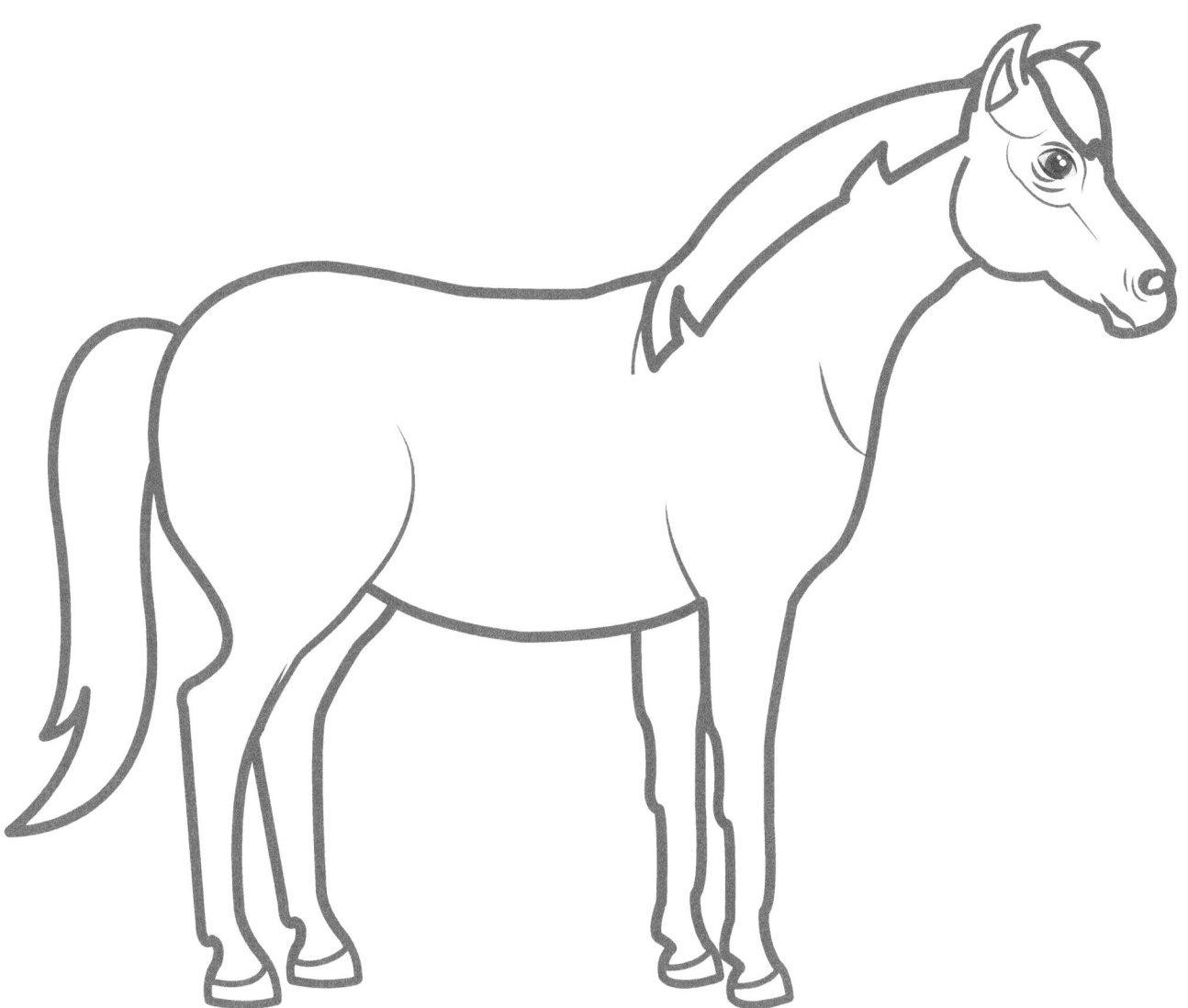

horse

Ii

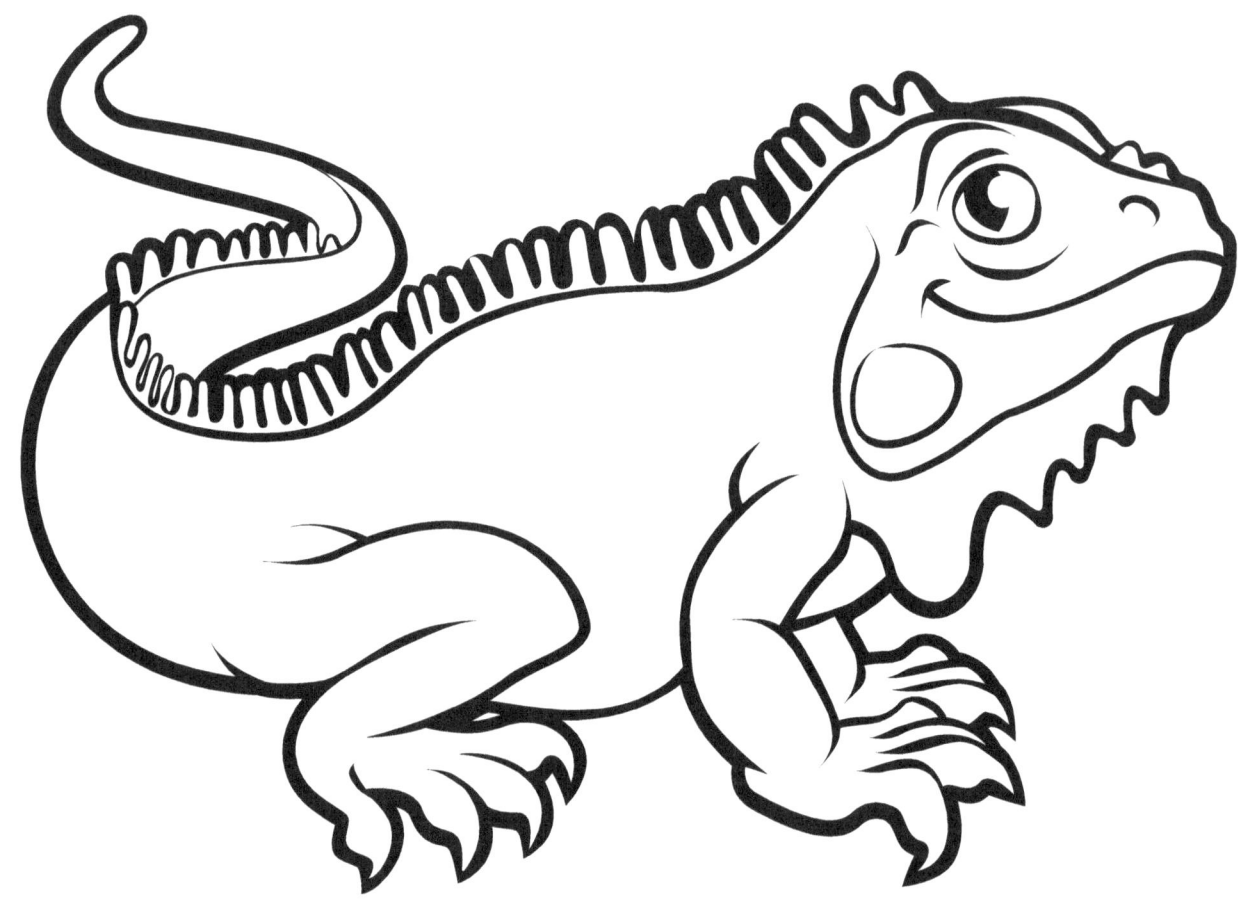

iguana

j

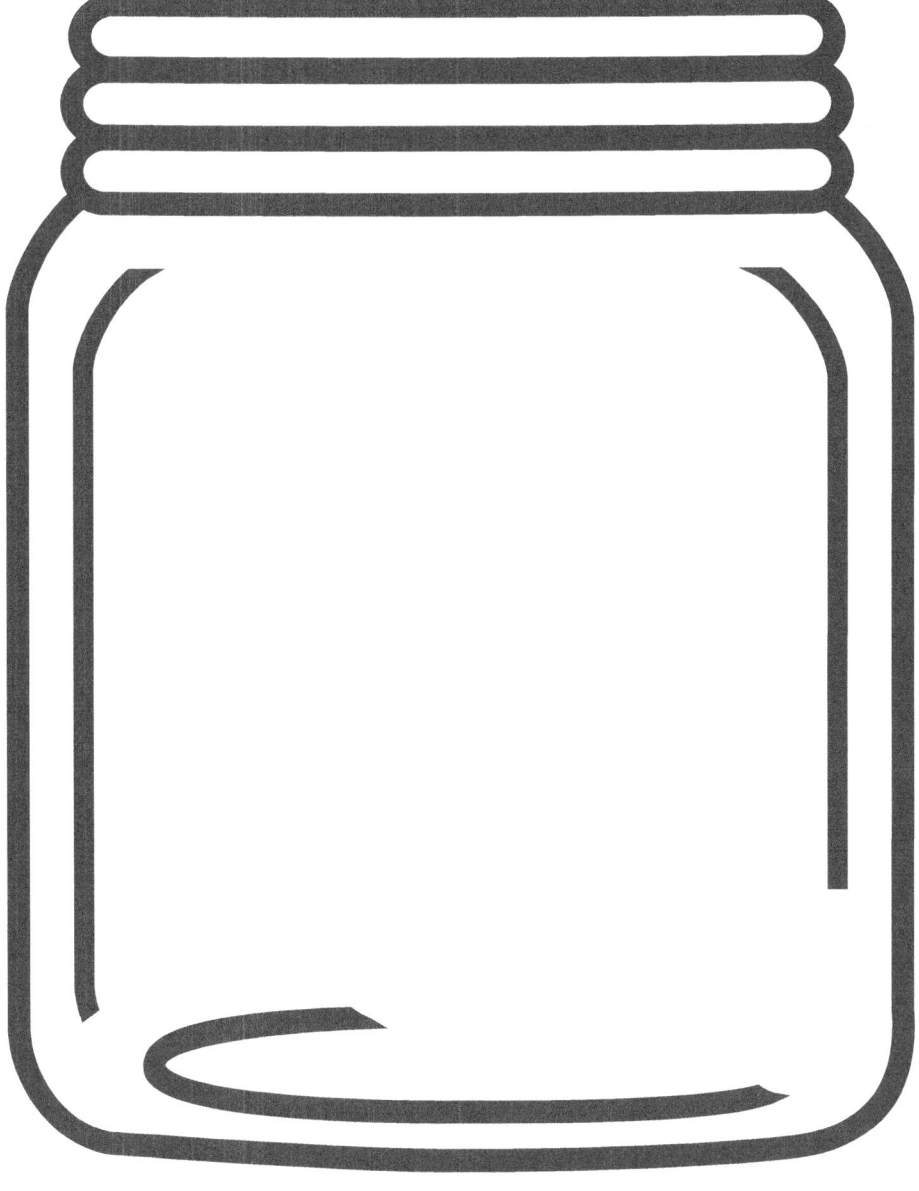

jar

Kk

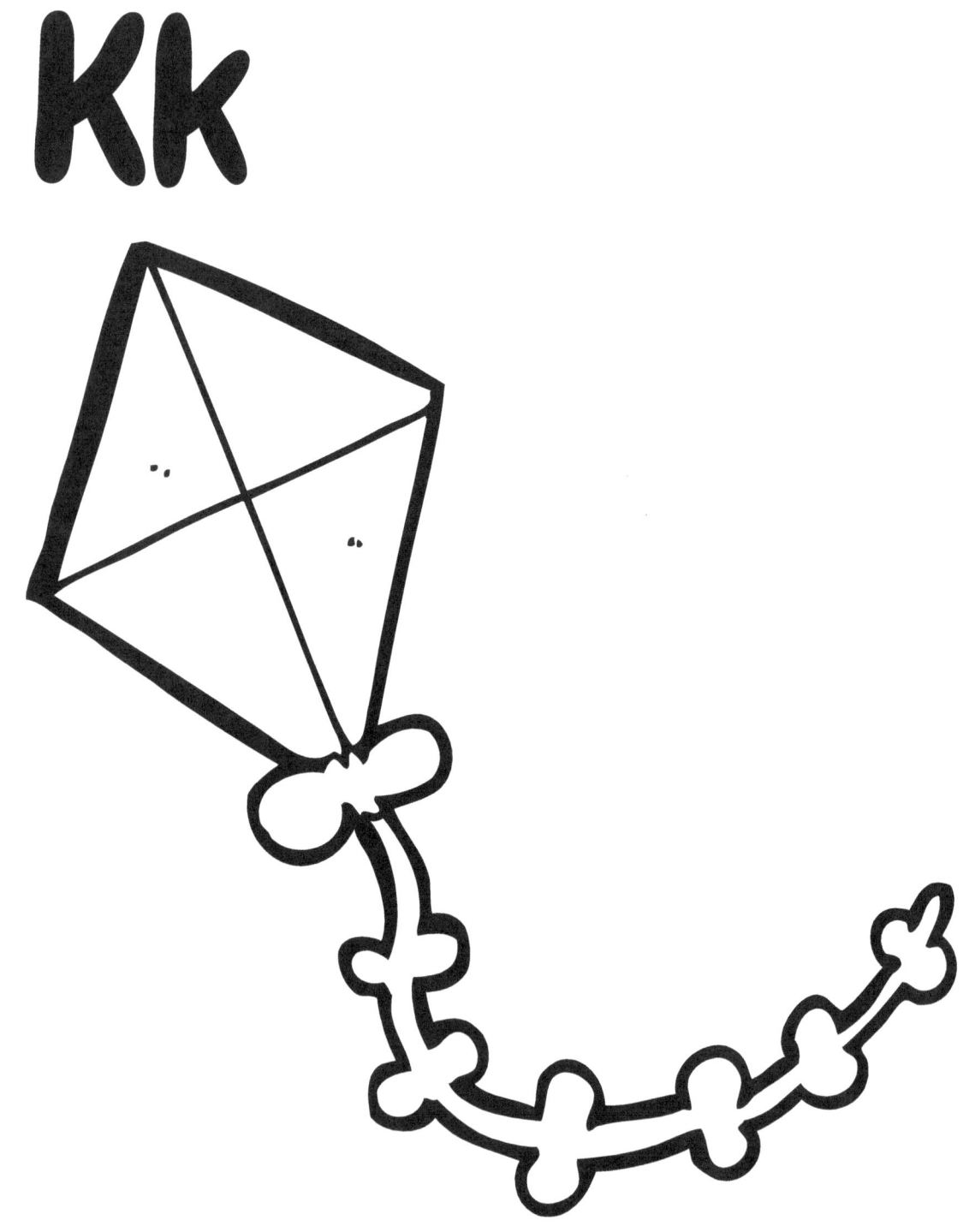

kite

Ll

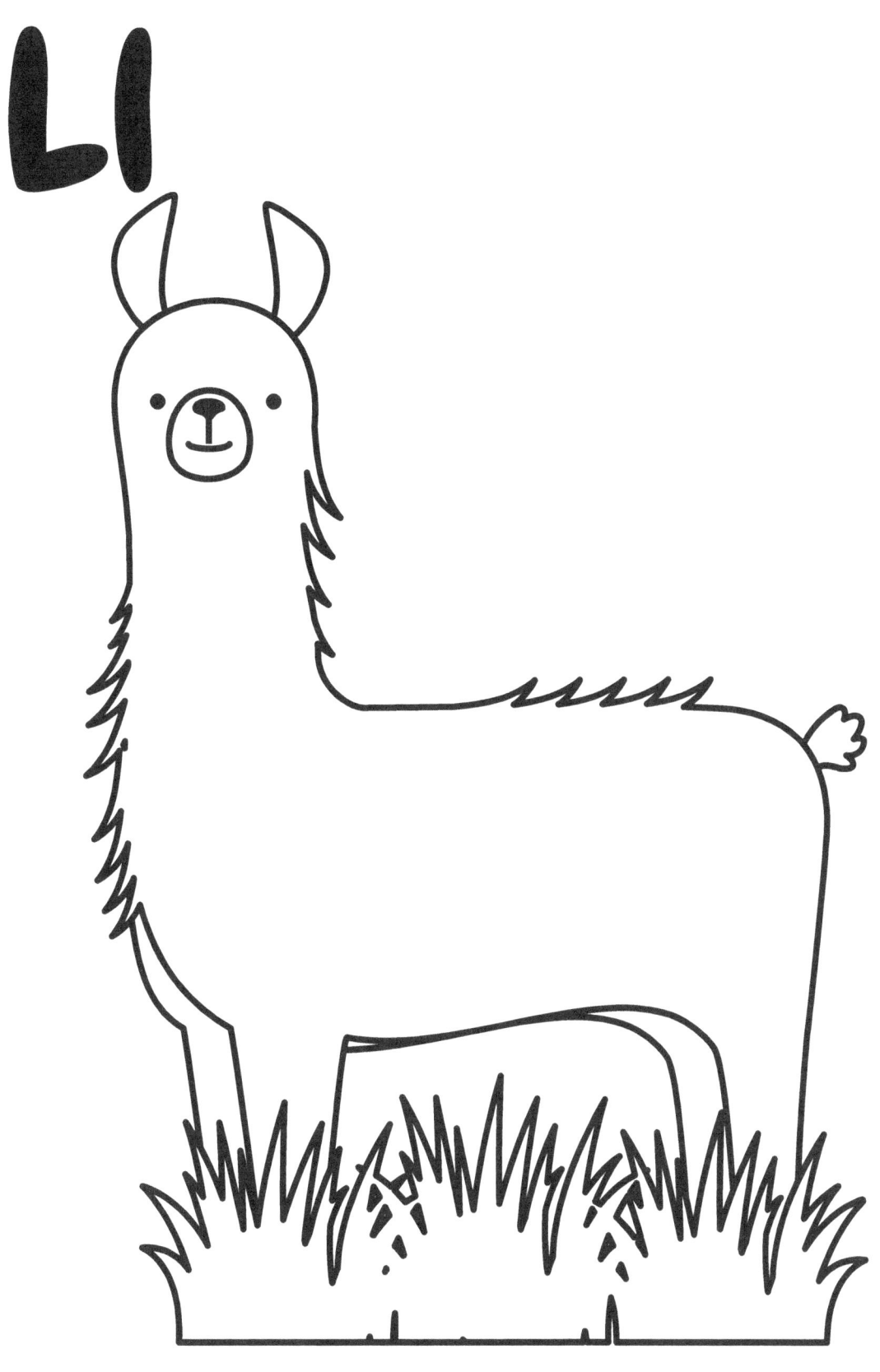

Llama

Mm

mouse

Nn

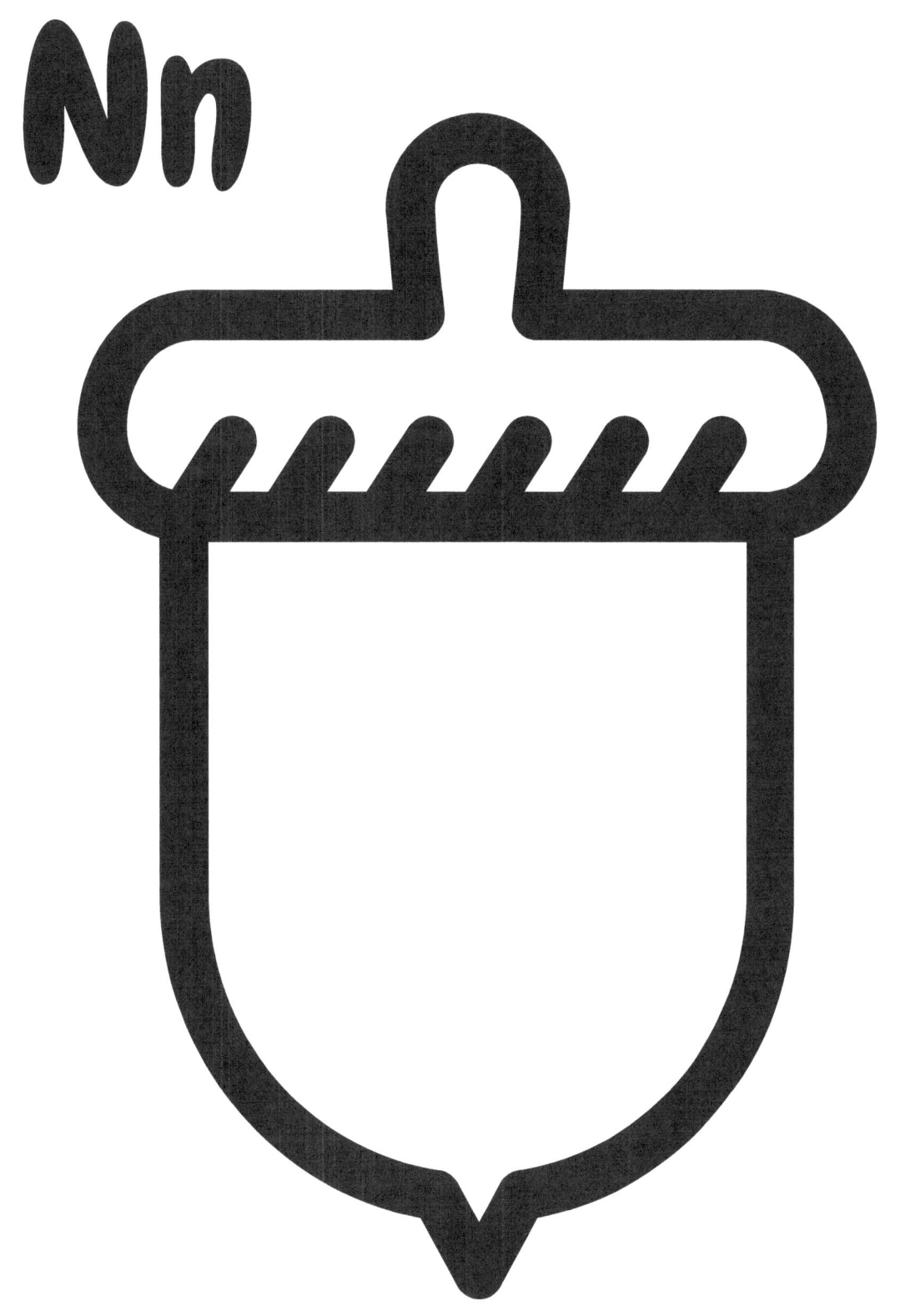

nut

Oo

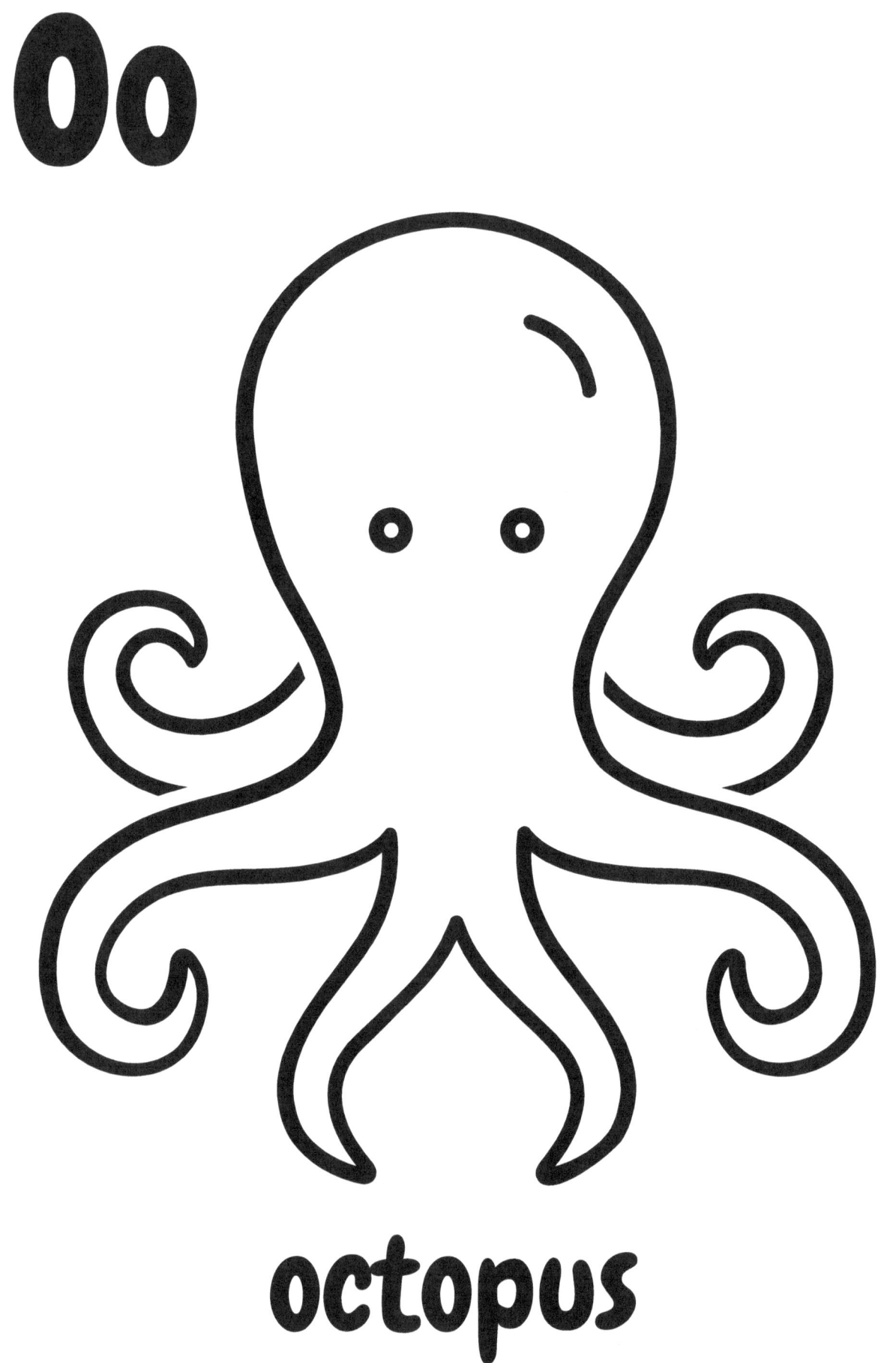

octopus

Pp

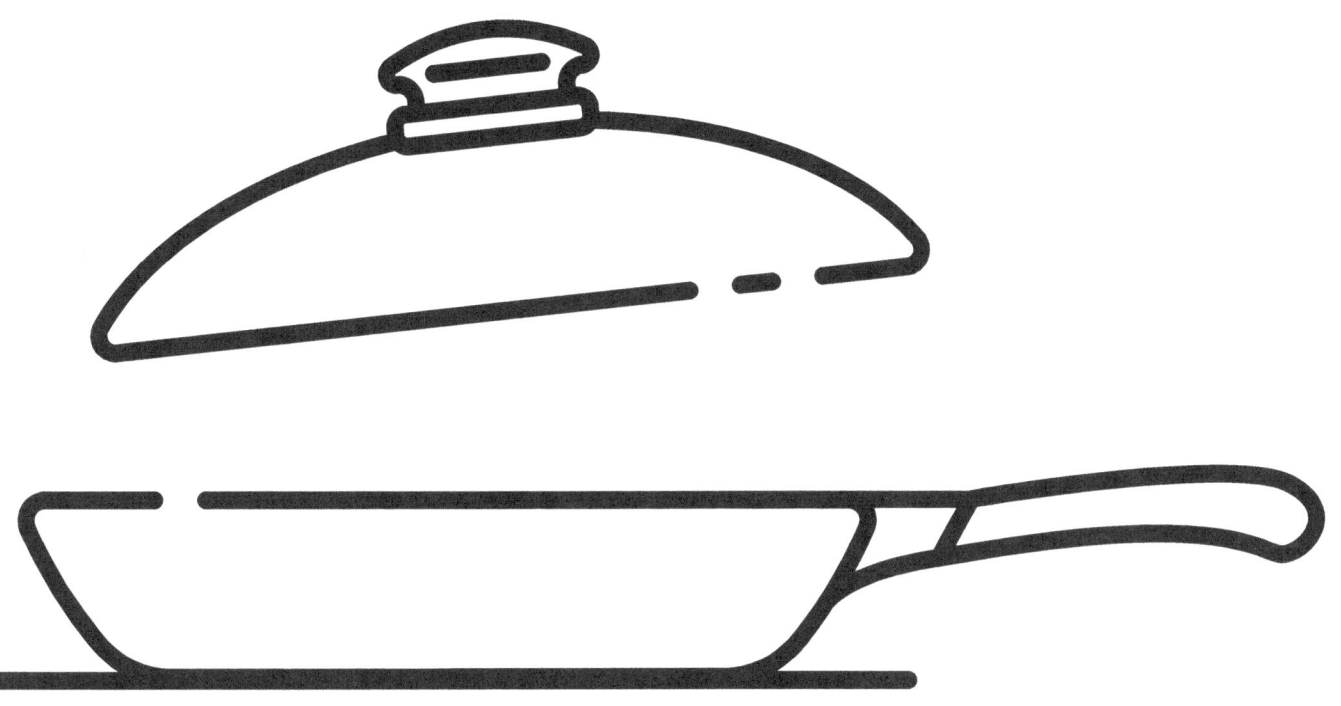

pan

Qq

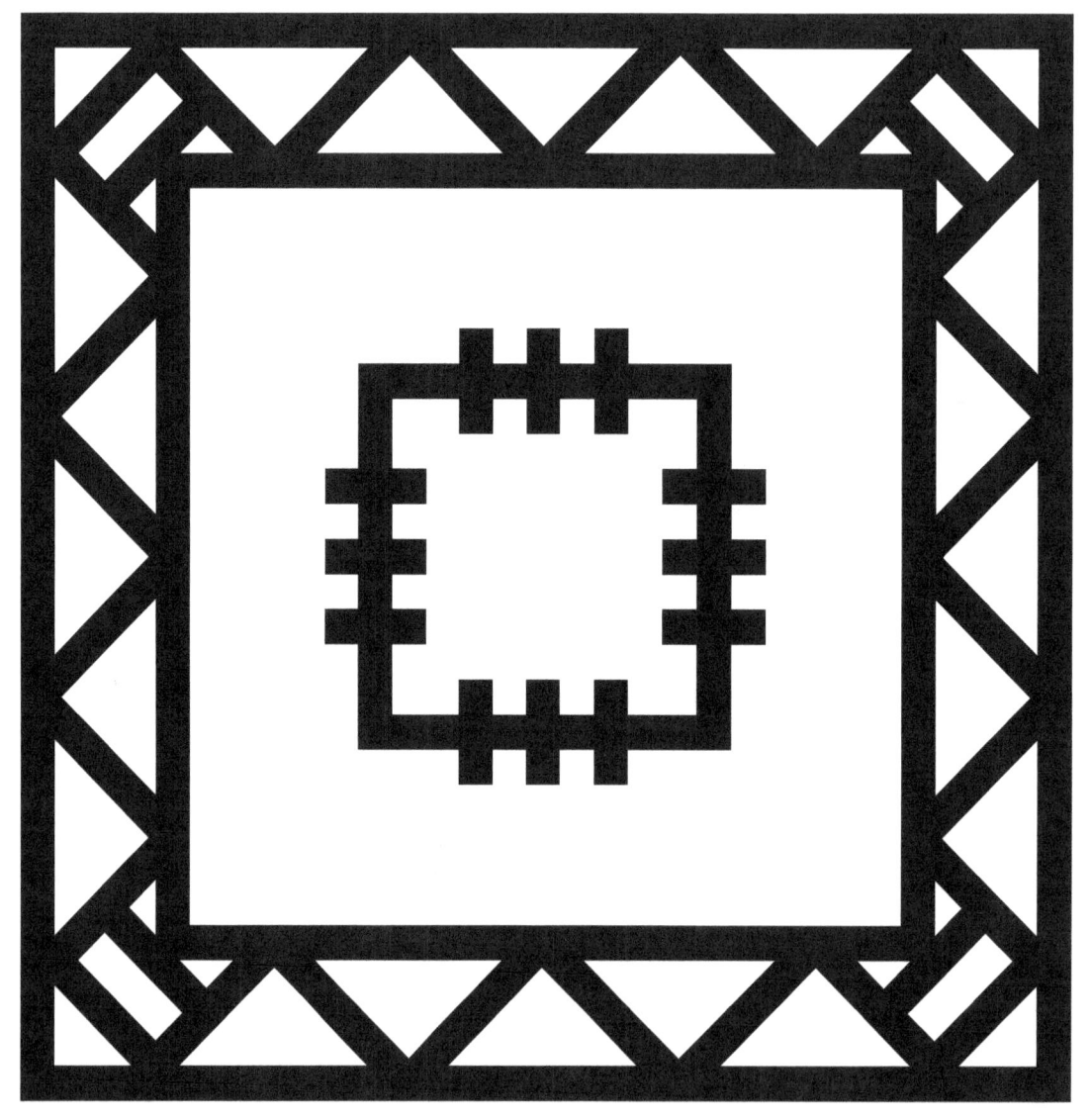

quilt

Rr

rat

Ss

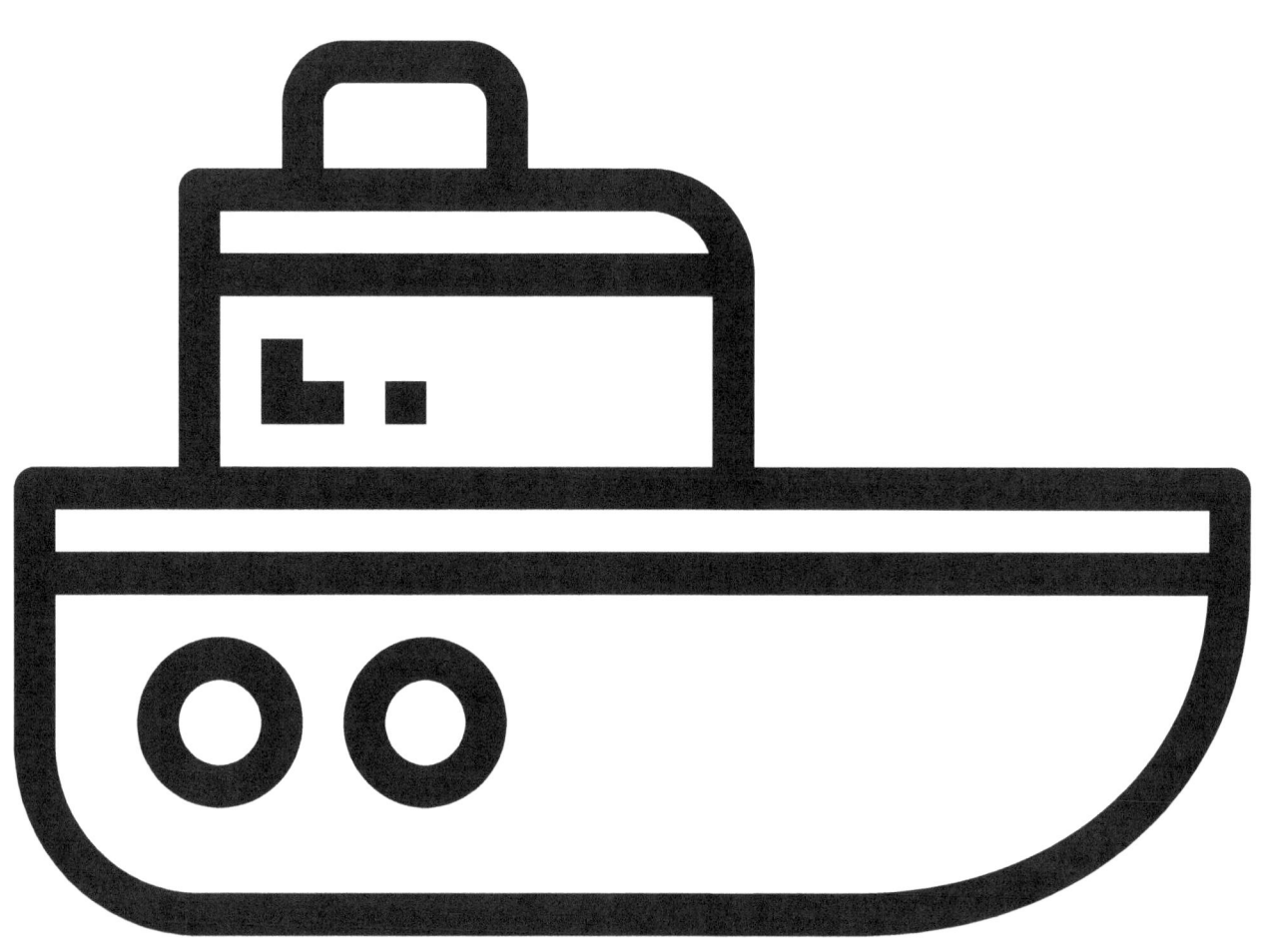

ship

Tt

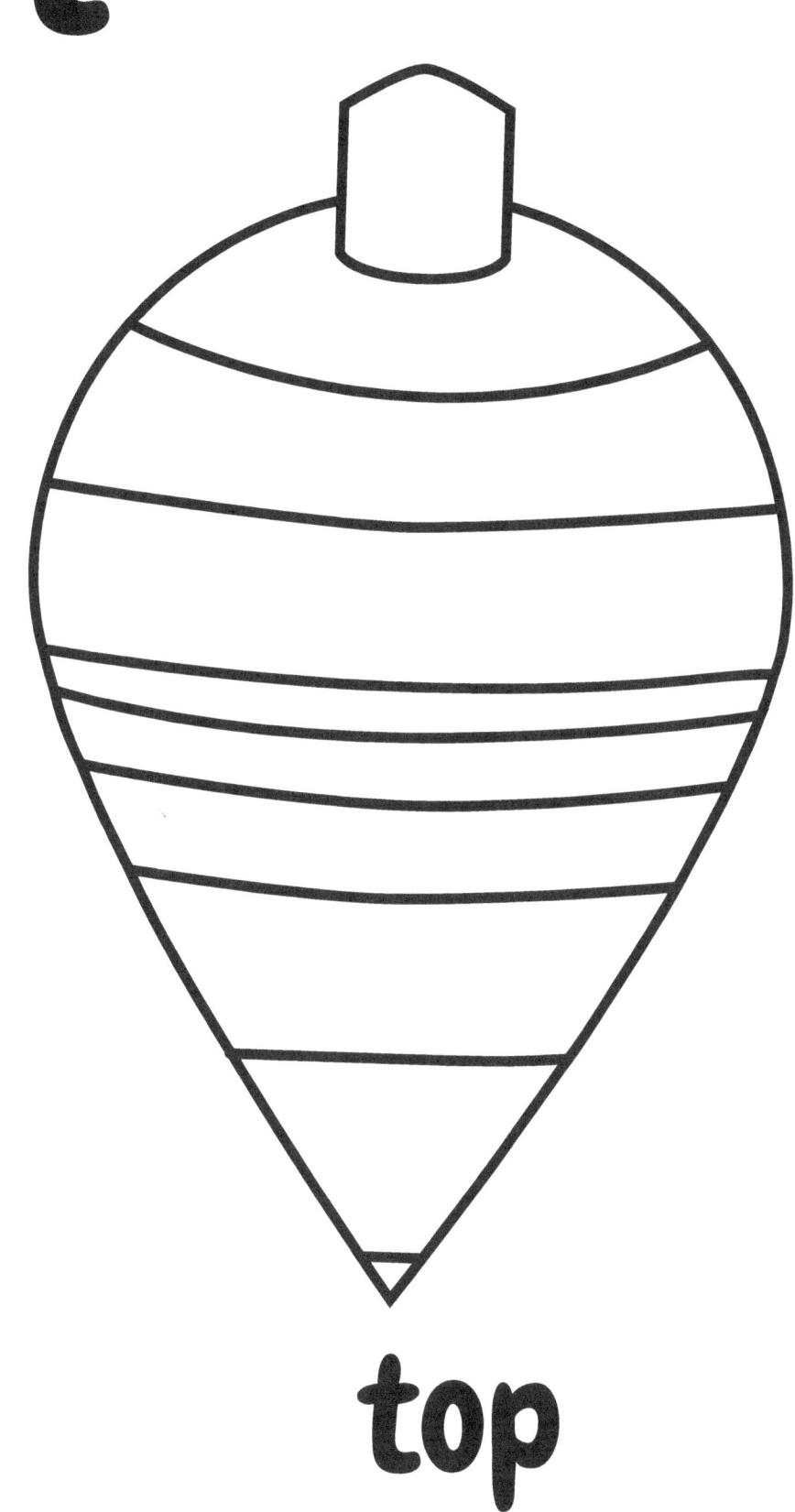

top

Uu

umbrela

Vv

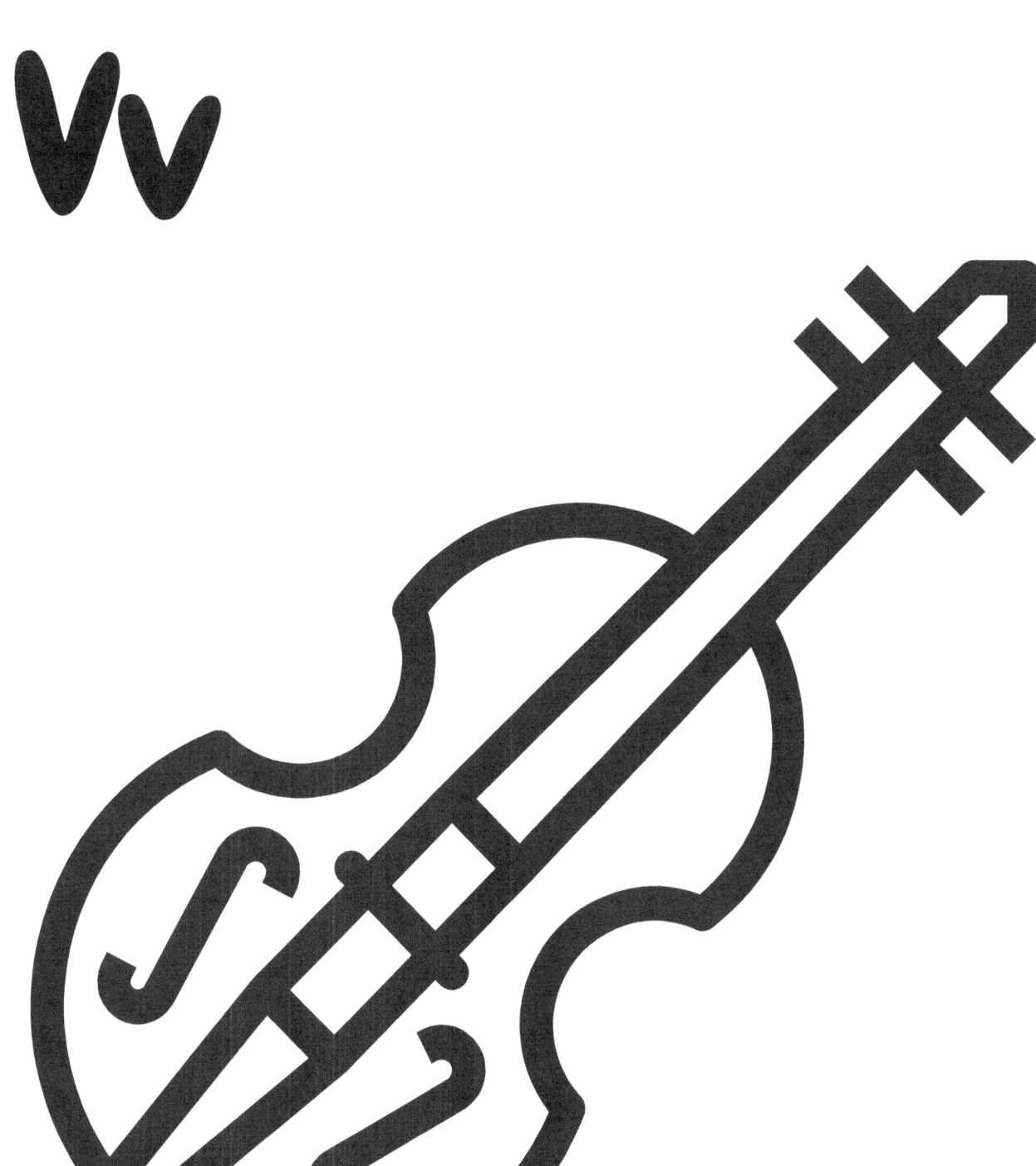

violin

Ww

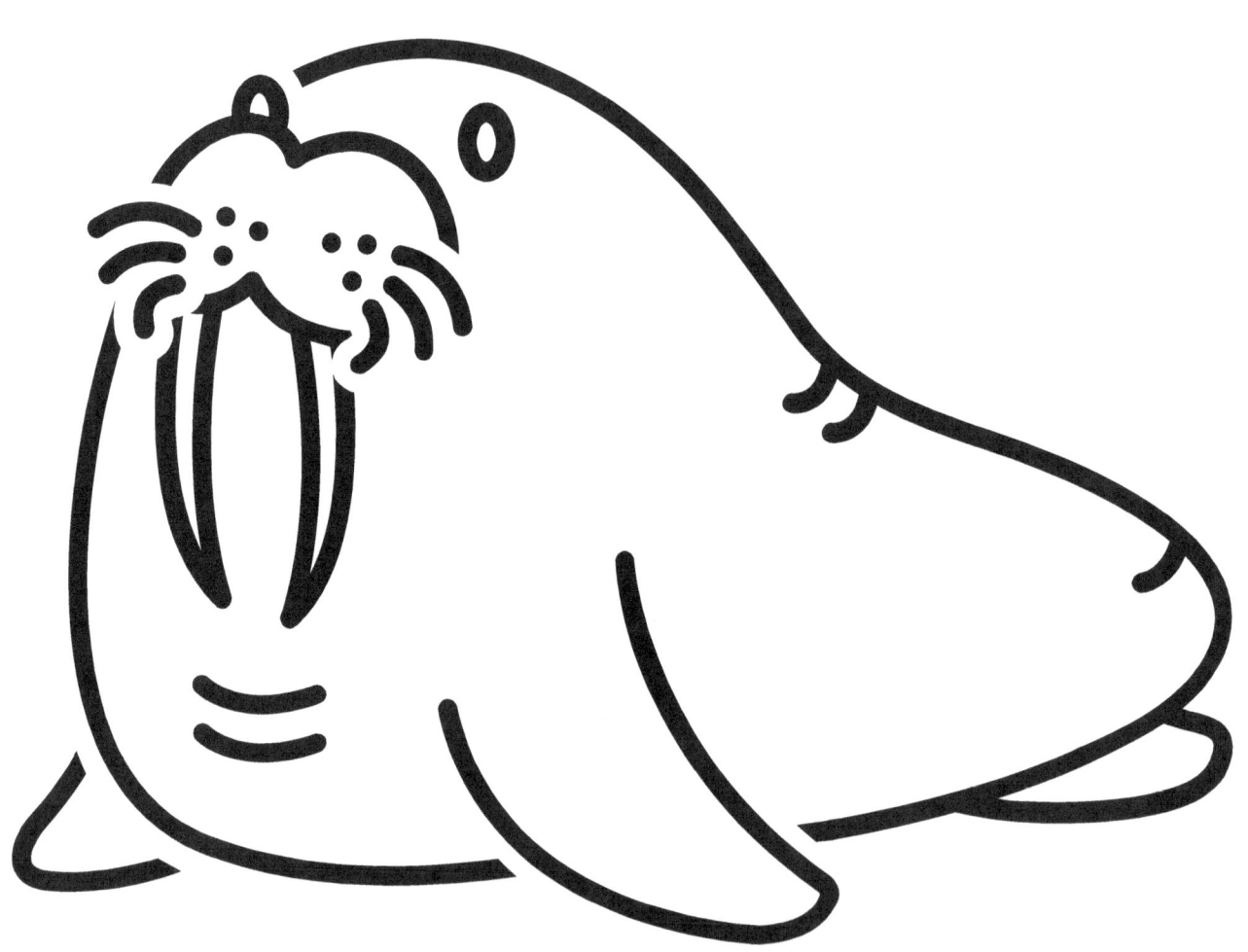

walrus

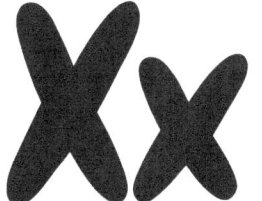

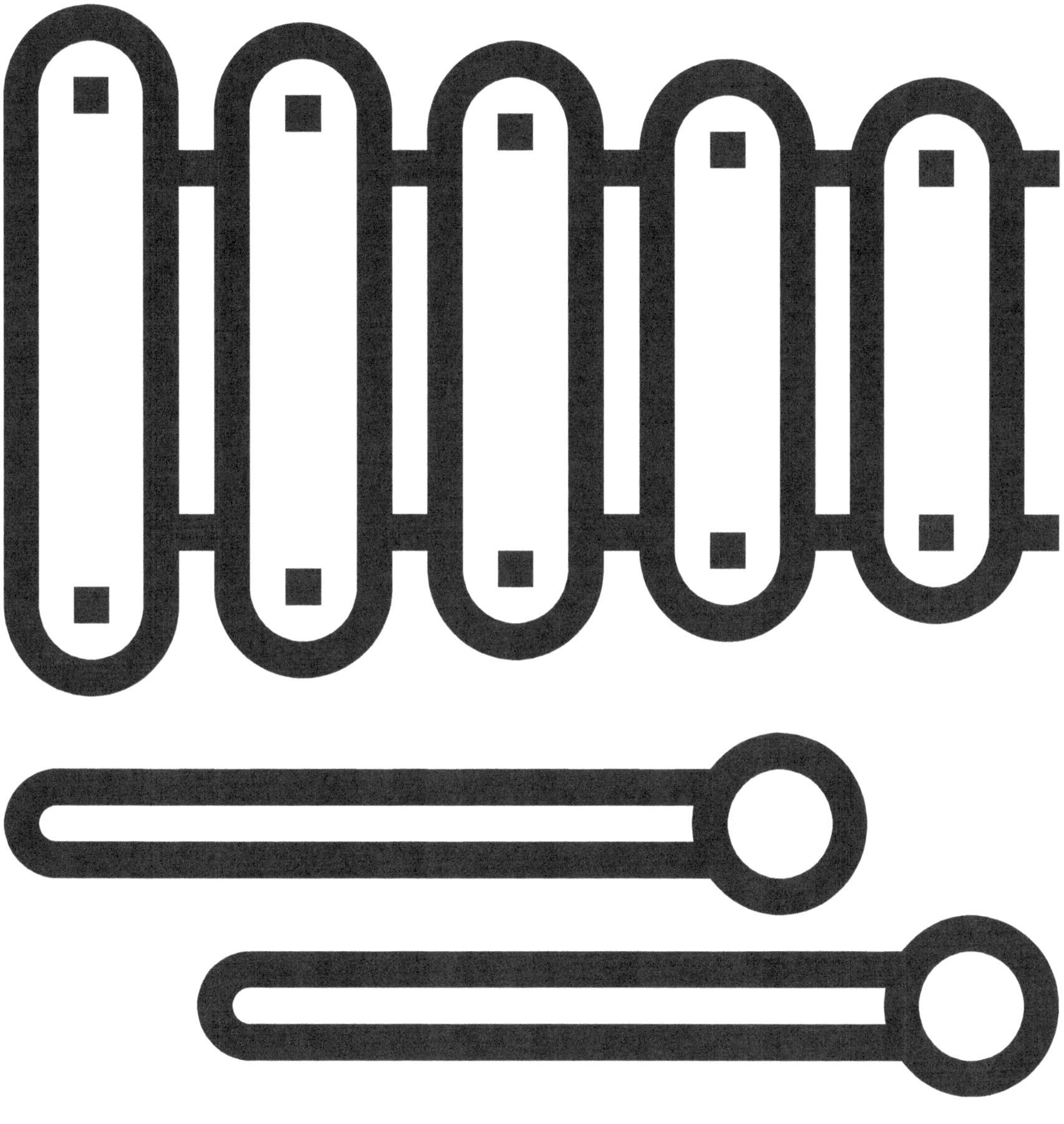

xylophone

Yy

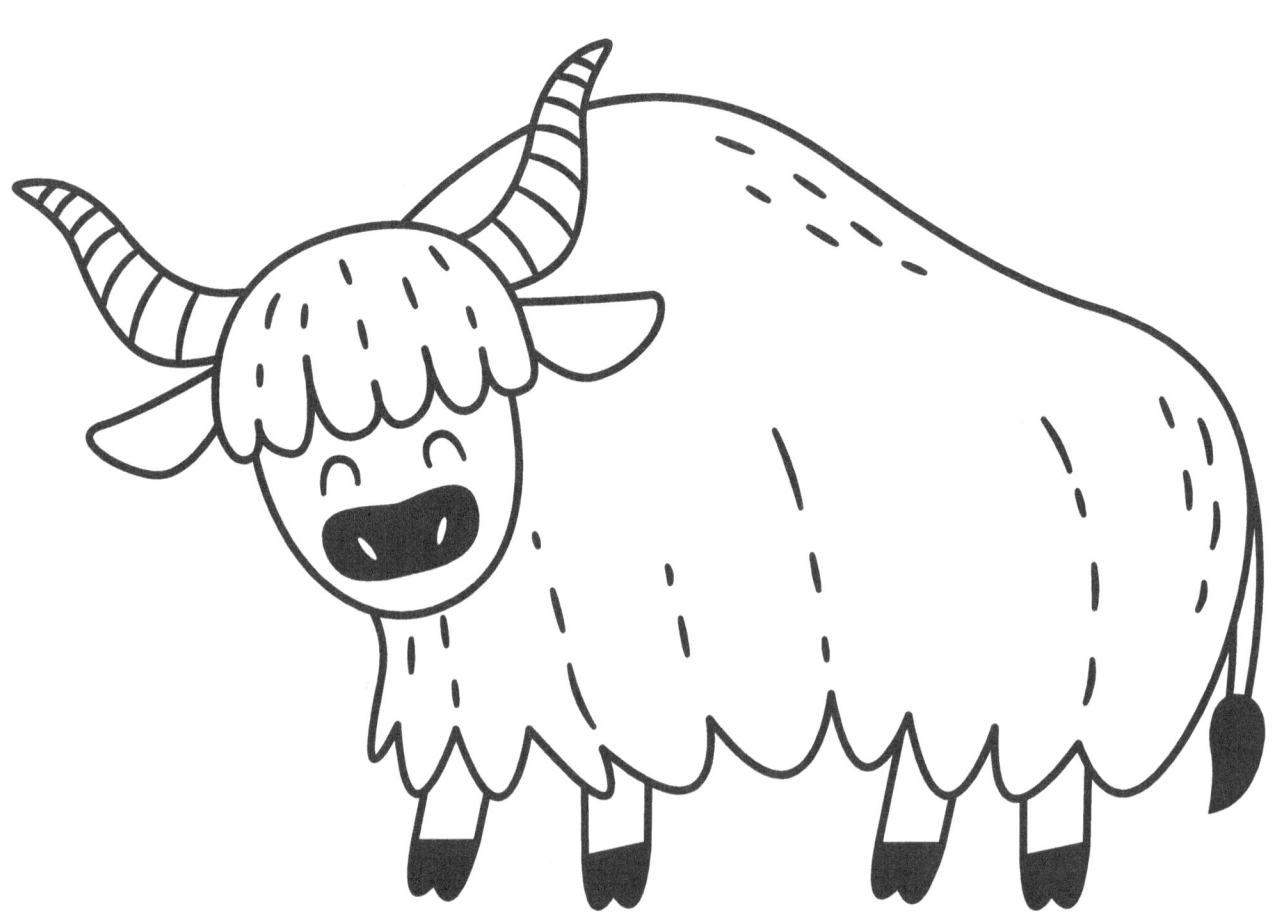

yak

Zz

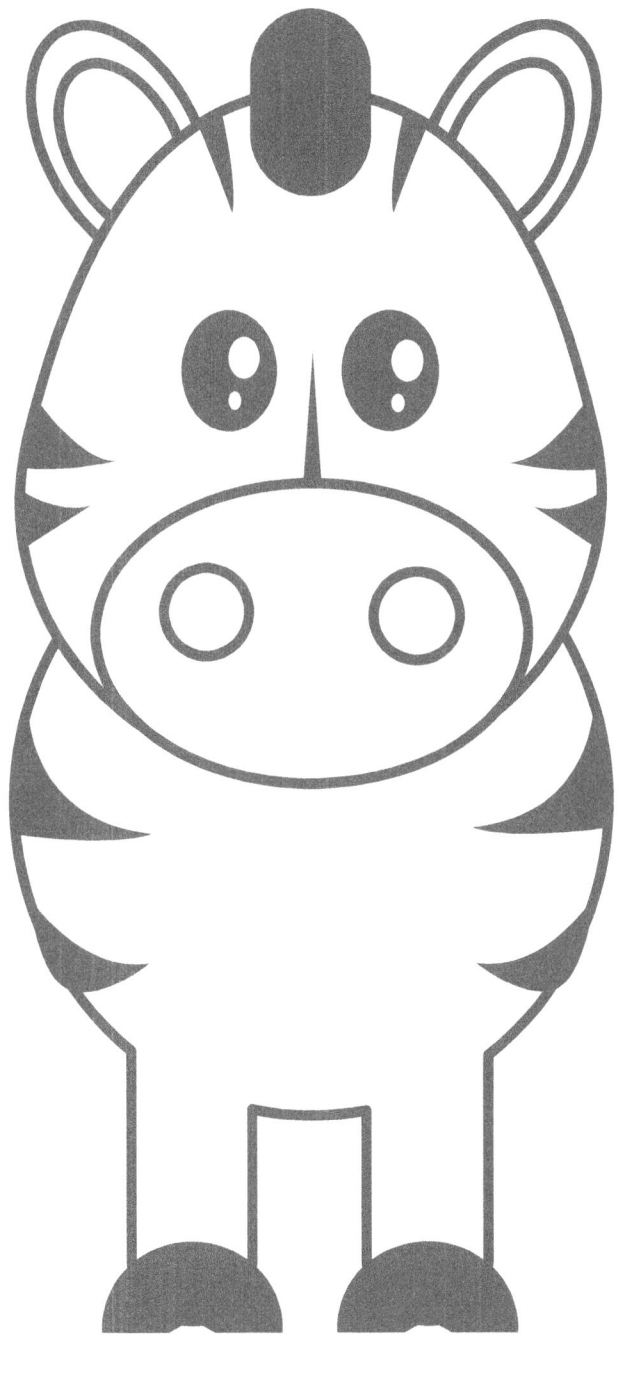

zebra

Reading

Sight words

—

see, sees, look, the, is are, a, run, come, this, him, go, I, we, too, it, my, am, in, here, like, said, at, and, you, up, can, me, on

Write each sight word on a 3x5 card. Use the cards like flash cards. When your child has memorized each word move on to the next page.

"at "word family

Read the end of the word first and then add the beginning sound.
"at" ...c
c...at= cat

cat

mat

fat

rat

bat

pat

gnat

sat

hat

The Cat

The cat sat.

He sat on the mat.

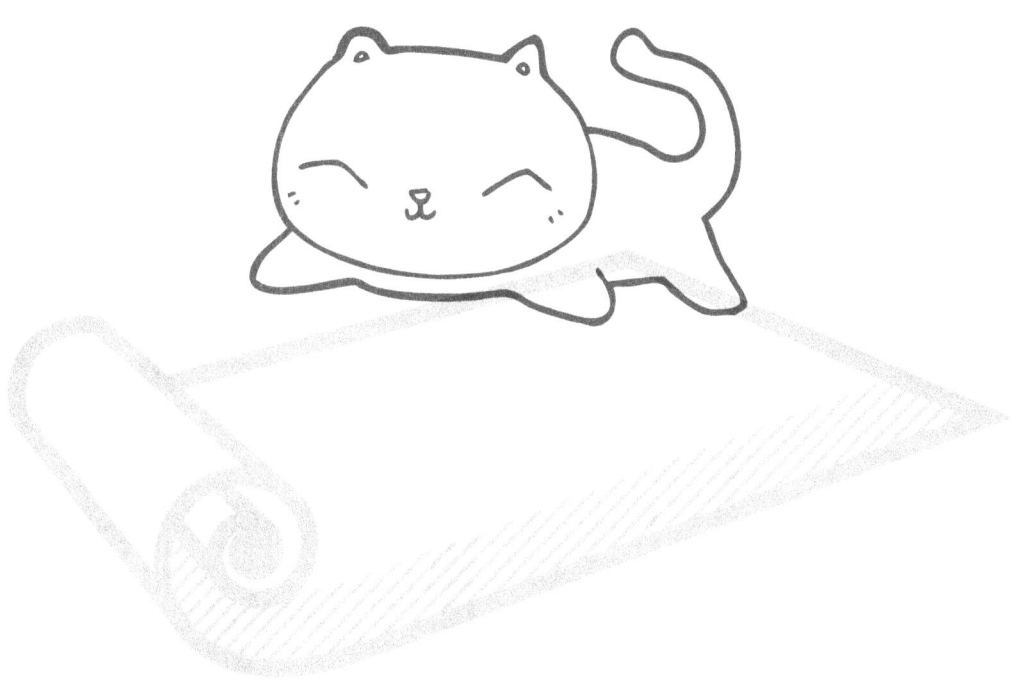

The cat sees the rat.

Run rat run.

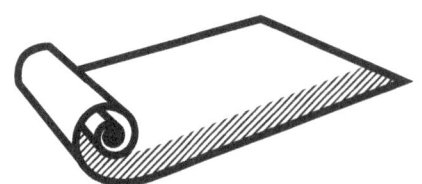

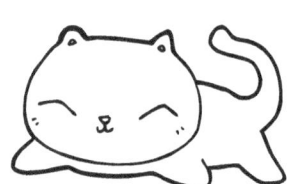

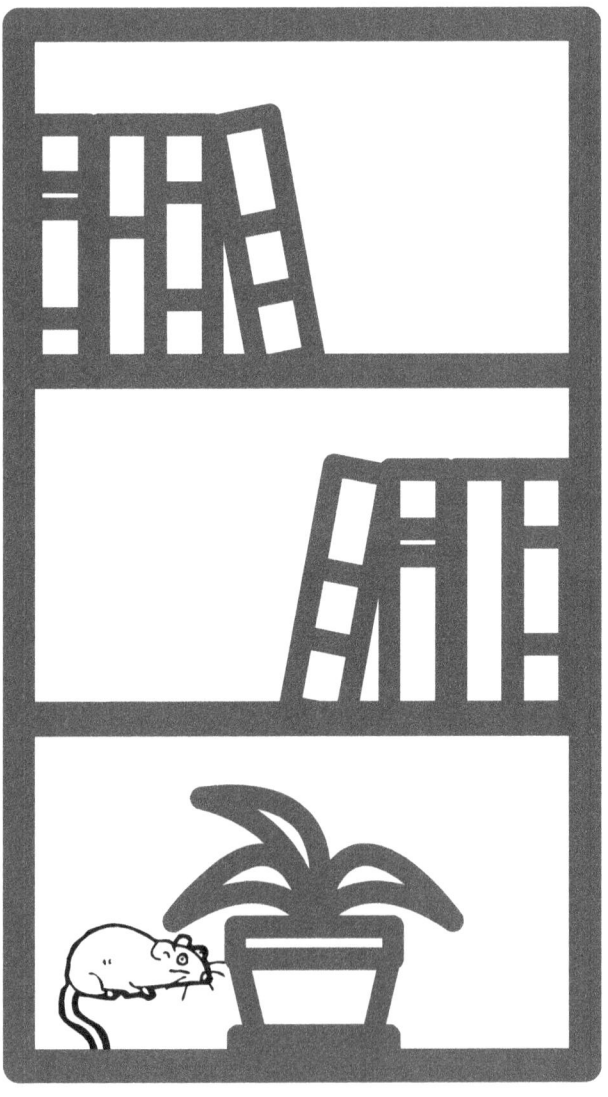

Run cat run.

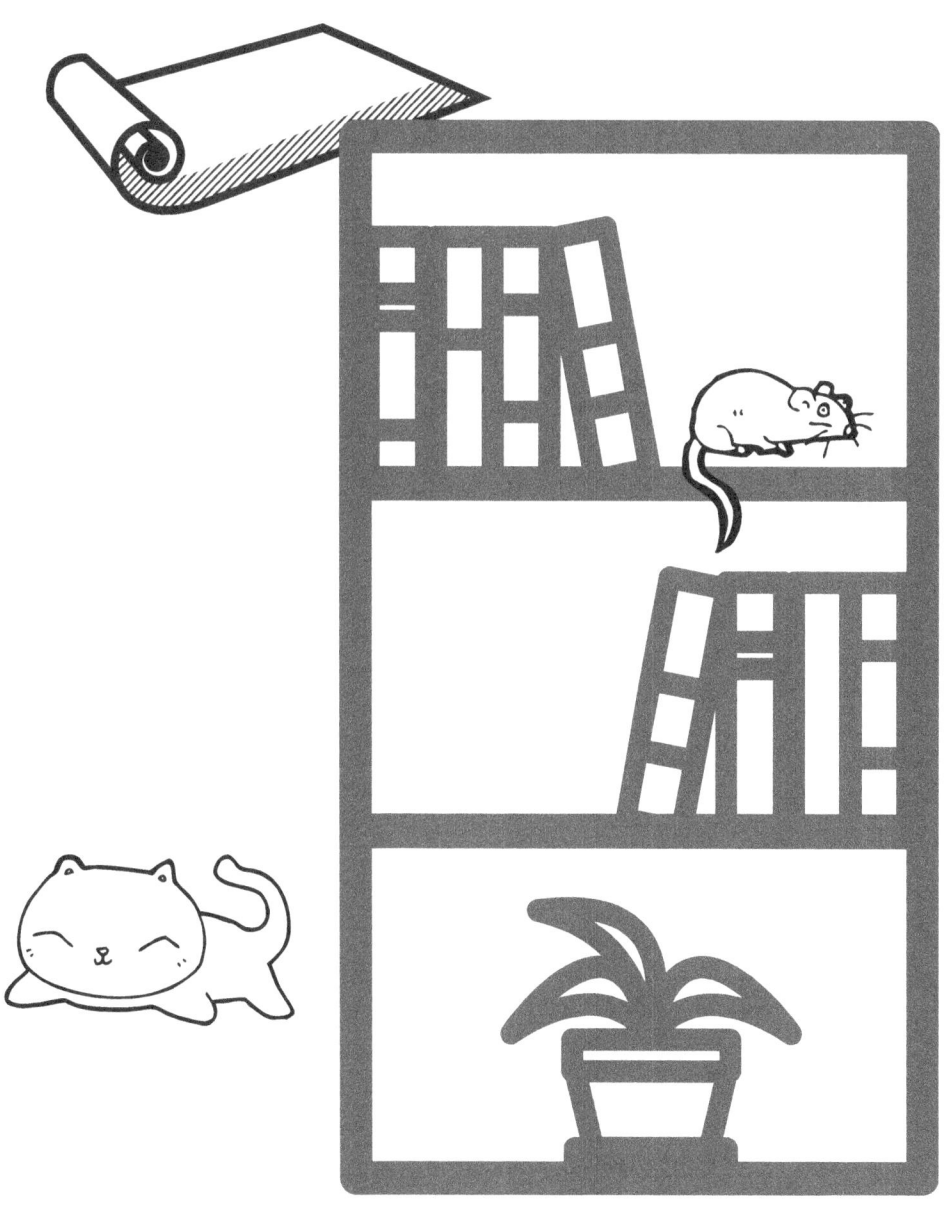

Thank you for choosing my book. I hope you like this book so much that you decide to purchase my other books--
My Baby's First Big Coloring Book--series
ABC's For You & Me
Happy Birthday, Jesus

Teach, Learn,& Grow Press